A Pilgrimage Small Group Resource

FITNESS KIT

Thom Corrigan

BRINGING TRUTH TO LIFE
NavPress Publishing Group
P.O. Box 35001, Colorado Springs, Colorado 80935

Pilgrimage Publishing, Hamilton, Massachusetts

Copyright © 1996 by Pilgrimage Publishing

All rights reserved. No part of this publication may be reproduced, stored in a retrieval system, or transmitted in any form by any means, electronic, mechanical, photocopy, recording, or otherwise, without the prior written permission of NavPress, P.O. Box 35001, Colorado Springs, CO 80935, except for brief quotations in critical reviews or articles.

The main Bible version used for Scripture quotations in this publication is *The Message: New Testament with Psalms and Proverbs* (MSG) by Eugene H. Peterson, copyright © 1993,1994, 1995, used by permission of NavPress Publishing Group. Other versions used include: the *HOLY BIBLE: NEW INTERNATIONAL VERSION®* (NIV®), Copyright 1973, 1978, 1984 by International Bible Society, used by permission of Zondervan Publishing House, all rights reserved; and the *New American Standard Bible* (NASB), © The Lockman Foundation 1960, 1962, 1963, 1968, 1971, 1972,1973, 1975, 1977.

ISBN 08910-99395
Library of Congress Catalog Card Number: 96-67605

Printed in the United States of America

1 2 3 4 5 6 7 8 9 10 11 12 13 14 15 / 00 99 98 97 96

Contents

Dedication

To Chris,
I am blessed each day by your loving care and support.

To my small group,
Thanks for modeling Christ's acceptance, commitment and encouragement.

The Key to Church Fitness May Be in Your Hands

Getting in shape has never been more popular, yet more elusive. Dozens of new diet strategies and exercise videos make their debut every year, trying to match the ceaseless demand. Yet we as a nation are schizophrenic about this: We enjoy the "runner's high," but overdose on junk food. We binge on aerobic exercise, then "channel surf" through life—without commitments or accountability to keep us fit.

Small groups keep us in shape

Obviously, there's more to fitness than eating sensibly, getting off our duffs, and getting regular exercise. Exercise researchers point out the need for an exercise strategy (based on duration and intensity) if we are to meet our fitness goals (good shape, long life, or true aerobic fitness.) We also need efficient fuel to run on, or we burn out. (We cannot fast all day and then sustain a 6:00 P.M. workout.)

Because physical fitness rewards individual effort, some try to live their Christian life the same way—all on individual effort. But fitness buffs also value the group. Reinforced by a common schedule and discipline, coupled with team effort and encouragement, people are getting and staying fit together.

Spiritual fitness relies on the same group dynamic— people get together, not to focus on their own efforts, but on God's grace and a deepening understanding of (and obedience to) God's Word. Indeed, the "small-group buzz" you hear across America is coming from breakfast nooks, brown bag lunches, and supper clubs and spreading to living rooms, locker rooms, and boardrooms.

With the longing for community being satisfied by the burgeoning small-group movement, and with much of our spiritual fitness now depending on small groups, this raises the question: Who is looking after the fitness of small groups, especially in the church?

How this book came to be

I wish this book had been available to me fifteen to twenty years ago when I was a struggling small-group leader. I graduated *summa cum laude* from the School of Hard Knocks. As I have grown in my ability to lead small groups, I have since encountered many situations when I could have used a trouble-shooting guide like this. Yet if it had not been for this prolonged learning curve, the small-group Fitness Kit would not have been written. As I took on larger roles as a pastoral overseer of many groups at four different churches, I kept looking for resources for myself and our leaders. The skills and insights packed into this book have been tried and tested under fire—in the churches I have served, as well as in a great number of ministries I have observed.

I have learned from many godly people who have been good role models, and from all the published works I could "beg, borrow or steal." I am indebted to a few people who have consistently supported me and encouraged me in developing this book: To my wife, my daughters, and office staff who covered for me so I could take the time to complete this. To Paul Santhouse and Steve Eames, who helped to develop the concept for Pilgrimage and who acted as the cheering squad. To John Winson, whose continuous love and commitment to our friendship and partnership has been an expression of God's grace to me. To Dick Peace, who challenges my heart and my mind to consider an ever-expanding picture. And to Karen Lee-Thorp, who has tutored and encouraged me. I hope I can be a real writer like you when I grow up. To Greg Kazanjian, a soldier in prayer. Thanks for being on your knees for me.

It takes more than communication skills to become an effective small-group leader or leader of a small-group ministry. Of utmost importance for the Kingdom of God is the heart of a leader. One measure of that is the willingness to take risks and to be available for God's use in any way.

Difficulties and setbacks in small groups are unavoidable, but I hope that some of my experiences will help you in dealing with yours. That's where this book will come in handy—to help you trouble-shoot what's happening and why, so that you can learn from your mistakes. But this Fitness Kit will have failed its purpose if it does not also encourage you in that most exciting, joyful and rewarding part of church life—being a small-group leader.

Chapter 1

Turning Small-Group Problems into "People Opportunities"

"God chooses what we go through.
We choose how we go through it."
—Victor Frankl, Holocaust survivor

"I like long walks, especially when they are taken
by people who annoy me."
—Fred Allen, realist

"If this sounds like some sort of science fiction horror story,
you should see the horror the 'comfort zone' wreaks on
people's lives."
—John Roger, pessimist

"I love the world, it's people I can't stand."
—Charlie Brown, optimist

People! As long as the church is made up of people like us, there will always be what optimists call "people opportunities."

The Bible records many cases of God's redeemed people arguing, fighting, conniving, misunderstanding, hurting, and abusing one another. God's people today still make mistakes, make a mess, or hurt one another. We do that to each other because people, redeemed or not, are human. God redeems and renews our fallen human nature, but that redemptive process is completed over time—through adversity and confrontation, through small groups and people opportunities. That's how God smooths out the rough edges of the Christian life: "As iron sharpens iron, so one man sharpens another" (Proverbs 27:17).

Let's look briefly at five problems that others bring into the small group. This will allow us to see how to turn those people problems into opportunities for growth. Then we'll look at two problems that we as leaders bring into the group that could be self-destructive.

The need to overcome Phariseeism

I grew up in a church which gave the impression that visitors or
inquirers needed to clean up their lives before we welcomed
them into our fellowship. This performance mentality is a deadly
form of the Phariseeism that Jesus continually railed against.
Wherever this smug attitude prevails—in a church, in a person, or
in a small group—it can spread like yeast leavening a lump of
dough and ruin Christian fellowship.

Jesus said to his disciples, "Be on your guard against the
yeast of the Pharisees and Sadducees" (Matthew 16:6). These
teachers and keepers of the law drew Jesus' ire because they
turned a spiritual relationship into religion. A life of keeping
laws, rules, and regulations is no "life" at all, but a slow spiritual death.

Many Christians do not cultivate the fruit that grows out of
being vitally connected to Christ. Even those in a position of
leadership, if they only talk a good game about Jesus but do
not enjoy a vital relationship with him, will eventually starve to
death spiritually. They are like the person who walks into a
classy restaurant, receives a beautiful menu—handwritten on
fine paper, with extensive, eloquent descriptions of the extra-
ordinary offerings—then proceeds to eat the menu!

Those who have never tasted of God's grace are no better
off than this menu-eater. Those who once had a relationship
based on God's grace, but have fallen back into ritualism or
religion, are even worse off (2 Peter 3:20-22). Just talking
about God in Christ, without experiencing the real thing,
doesn't cut it. If the richness of a daily walk with Jesus is a
foreign experience to some in your group, be sure to introduce them to the real thing. Don't let them leave the group
having only sampled the menu.

The need to overcome an us-and-them attitude

This inability to appropriate God's grace in our lives, not only
leads to a Phariseeism which is incompatible with the gospel,
but lends itself to an us-and-them attitude that kills the
church. Some churches have a fortress mentality that seeks
to protect us by making it hard for them to enter. "Them" is
anyone who needs to jump through religious hoops, apart
from grace, in order to become part of "us."

This religious mentality stifles small-group life by closing
the door to any form of evangelism, outreach, or service

(except to perpetuate its own kind). I have found that when Phariseeism infects a small group, admitting faults to one another is harder to do, and reconciliation between groups is rarely considered.

Not only are we saved by the grace extended by a loving Father through the sacrifice of his only Son, but we live by grace as our daily bread. That daily, life-saving grace is the antidote to religious ritualism, legalism, and Phariseeism. This grace will also stir up a hunger for spiritual reality and for relationships with the new people God brings to your group.

Because "the heart is deceitful above all things, and desperately wicked" (Jeremiah 17:9), our best hope for reconciled relationships is hearts that are healed and minds that are renewed in the image of Christ. Your love, compassion, and honesty could shame others out of their us-and-them mentality.

Confrontation may not be necessary unless other group members are being hurt. Admitting your own bias, bigotry, or brokenness could set an example. If you have bias of any kind—against couples who divorce, parents whose teens are out of control, fat people who lose control of their bodies—confess it.

If Phariseeism appears in your group, turn your experience with adversity and diversity into a parable of grace for the benefit of others.

The need to overcome selfishness

People are basically selfish. We are products more of our culture than of Christ. Our culture emphasizes personal rights over community responsibilities. Our culture overlooks the good of others and insists on "looking out for number one," including suing anyone who "violates" our rights.

The church is comprised of these selfish people. Investing time, energy, or money in our own recreation seems to be more important than investing time, energy or money in the kingdom of God. Given such skewed priorities group members may be unable or unwilling to reach out to each other outside of group time, let alone to others in the church or their neighborhoods.

This prevailing problem calls us to practice a lifestyle of charity and humility. By adopting the mind of Christ, we can know what it means to "do nothing out of selfish ambition or vain conceit, but in humility consider others better than yourselves" (Philippians 2:3). Some things are better "caught than taught," and this attitude is one of them. You can expose your group to Scriptures dealing with "one another," and pray for the mind of Christ to overcome selfishness, but equally important will be the example they have seen in you.

The need to overcome critical "defeatists"

Another common problem that turns up in groups concerns the skeptics or defeatists. They hail from the *We've-never-done-it-that-way-before* school of thought, or from the dead-end street of *That-will-never-work*. Their needling and "wet blanket" remarks not only dampen enthusiasm but seem to challenge our right to lead or to speak. If left uncontested, their challenge undermines the confidence other people have in our leadership and in the direction the group is headed.

I believe the best way to respond to negative thinkers is with Scripture passages that emphasize faith and hope. "Now faith is being sure of what we hope for and certain of what we do not see" (Hebrews 11:1). Remind your group members, as did Jesus, that the only "constant" is change itself. Jesus continually challenged the status quo. With parables of the kingdom, such as the parable of the new wineskins (Luke 5:36–38), Jesus brought about the new life he talked about. The Christian life is a walk of faith, and God will continually confront us with new experiences, so that we might learn to trust him with more and more of our life.

The need to overcome "self-made" individualists

Another type of person who presents a problem to most groups is the self-achieving independent person. Such persons have made their own way, pulled themselves up by their own bootstraps (so they think), and pushed past all obstacles. Don't confuse this person with someone who is highly motivated and goal-oriented. The difference is in the attitude of the heart.

Self-made individualists don't think they need you or anyone else in their life. They often have another agenda, maybe one outside their awareness, or one from their past they've suppressed. Deep inside they may have been scarred by broken trust and unreconciled relationships. What the small group awakens in them—and what they have yet to experience—is their need to have their heart touched by God and their need for honest relationships in community.

You can have an immense impact on these individualists if you will love them, no matter what they do or say. You might have to prove that you are on their side, but in the long run, love and consistency will prevail.

The apostle Paul summarizes this paradox of what to do with people who are so problematic yet so necessary for your group to grow: "For the sinful nature desires what is contrary to the Spirit, and the Spirit what is contrary to the sinful nature. They are in conflict with each other, so that you do not do what you want" (Galatians 5:17). We are imperfect people who need the ongoing work of salvation and reconciliation. And you have been invited to participate in that wonderful process. It's called Life in Small Groups!

;o, you need (and are) people who have problems!

A group without problems is hard to believe. Like the couple who claims their married life is devoid of any disagreement, we must ask ourselves, Were they ever really married? If a couple does not feel safe enough to let down their guard and reveal who they really are, in what sense are they married? Likewise, if your group claims to have no problems, you should wonder, *Are they even breaking the surface?*

I believe that small groups need to get to the level of "storming," that is, when we move from *formation* and *normalized* relationships (where everyone learns how to be "nice" to one another), through *crises* and *confrontations,* to a place of *real honesty.* Once there, we can say in all honesty, "I do not agree with you," or "I don't like it when you do that."

This storming level is also called "speaking the truth in love" (Ephesians 4:15). That's when God does some wonderful work of reconciliation and restoration in our group. When we honestly work through stormy problems, the group will likely enter a time of greater productivity in building relationships and community.

We leaders also bring our own problems to our groups. Isn't it wonderful? As well-educated, trained, or experienced as we may be, there are areas of our life that the Lord may want to work in. This can be threatening because many of us have been taught *not* to let down our guard and *not to* let others get too close.

Such thinking runs contrary to Scripture. Jesus lived with and taught a group of 70 people, but spent more time with the Twelve, and even more with three apostles in particular—James, Peter, and John (who enjoyed a closer relationship with Jesus). Evidently, even our Lord needed close fellowship with a few others.

We leaders need a small group for the same reasons as Jesus, but with the additional reason that we are sinful and need the group to deal with two problems most prevalent among small-group leaders.

The need to be in control

Most leaders feel a need to be in control. We like to keep things nice and neat. But this outlook grabs us at the very point where we need to let go: *If we are going to have successful small-group ministries, we must release appropriate amounts of control and responsibility to people we have selected, invested in, and equipped to lead in some capacity. But in doing so, we run into control problems.*

We fear being out of control. We speak of controlling forest fires, teenagers, tempers, thoughts, actions, feelings, and destinies. When we are out of control we feel powerless, overwhelmed, and helpless. We fear being out of control and losing control—of ourselves and others. As we struggle to find new ways to regain control, we may explode with verbal violence against ourselves or others. Or we may feel a bit paranoid—even paralyzed, and develop any number of stress-related illnesses.

Obviously some control, however minor it may seem, is critical to our health and well-being. Unfortunately, the greatest stressor of all is one we have no control over whatsoever, and it tends to drive us crazy. We cannot prepare enough for it, respond quickly enough to it, or adapt our thinking and behavior enough to "handle" it.

This stressor is called CHANGE—rapid, troublesome, unsettling, uncontrollable CHANGE. Change is a creation of our God. He put into motion a system of continual change: Day into night into day . . . spring into summer into fall into winter . . . water into ice into water into vapor.

We can readily acknowledge and appreciate our inability to control seasonal change. Why then do we think we can control other aspects of change with godlike expenditures of time and energy, all in the name of protecting the status quo? Is it possible that we, too, hail from the *We've-never-done-it-that-*

way-before school of thought, or from the dead-end street of
That-will-never-work?

e fear of failure

Another problem that leaders bring to a group manifests
itself in various ways, some very subtle. Imagine this all-too-
common scenario:

> You go to the home of the group host, or maybe you host
> the group yourself. You set up chairs and make sure every-
> thing is in order. You greet each person who arrives, intro-
> ducing any newcomers to the regulars, and vice versa. You
> open in prayer, make necessary announcements, lead with
> an appropriate ice-breaker, and share some personal his-
> tory. Next you turn to the Bible, read the selected passage,
> teach from a prepared outline, and answer any questions
> that arise. You then ask if anyone needs prayer, especially
> on issues related to that day's topic, and pray accordingly.
> After closing the meeting, over coffee and cookies, you
> attempt to touch base with each person who attended.

So, you say, *Where is the problem? We covered every necessary part of group life tonight. Right?*

Well, yes, but with one little difference. It wasn't we, it
was I. The problem here is just that: *I DID IT.* We leaders
bring the problem of our ego to a group. If I am one part of
the group, which is functioning as a microcosm of the greater
Body of Christ, then we have a wonderful picture of the
church as described by the apostle Paul in 1 Corinthians 12.
("Now the body is not made up of one part but of many. . . .
As it is, there are many parts, but one body.")

The problem is not in doing all of the tasks, but in our
concept of leadership—thinking or feeling we must be in control in order to complete those tasks. The root of this problem
is often a fear of failure and may be based on viewing our
Father as a demanding and relentless taskmaster. If we see
God that way, then we will attempt to do everything perfectly.
But if our view of God is of a loving, merciful Father who is
behind us no matter what, then we will stop worrying and
start delegating because we want to bring glory to him.

The difference is in how we see God and respond to him.
When I see God as merciful and just, then I am not afraid of
punishment, but rather look to him for encouragement and

grace to go on. I can then invite others to put their hand to the plow, and encourage them in acts of service. I know that they will make mistakes and may "fail." But through the lens of grace and mercy, I see them as future leaders and coworkers who can benefit from my experience and understanding. My problem then becomes a matter of prayer before God and allowing him to deal with it.

Check-Up Quiz

Dealing with issues of control and failure

Here's a chance to examine your need to control and your fear of failure.

1. In your group, have you reached the level of storming (a place of real honesty), or are you still learning how to be "nice" to one another? Is your group somewhere in between?

2. When do you feel powerless, overwhelmed, or helpless?

3. When, if ever, have you exploded with verbal violence against yourself or others?

4. Are you showing any signs of stress-related illnesses: lapses in concentration, obsessions with work, loss of your usual interests or friendships, irritable behavior, emotional anxiety, or "accidental" injuries?

Paradoxically, we must conclude that small groups need people who have problems and are led by people with problems. Otherwise, you have no group members, no leaders, and no need for the group—or God! Let's adopt a leadership style that allows for growth, change, and health. The rest of the tools in the fitness kit will help you do that.

Chapter 2

Attitudes and Assumptions that Prevent or Respond to Problems

*"For the thing I greatly feared has come upon me,
and what I dreaded has happened to me."*
—**Job, survivor of family tragedy**

*"People tend to become what the most important people
in their lives think they will become."*
—**John Maxwell**

*"Leaders can be, when they choose,
significant bearers to the spirit."*
—**Max DePree**

I believe our attitudes and assumptions are the key to preventing many problems that turn up in small-group life. I have found that certain attitudes and assumptions shape my success or failure.

*ssumption 1: God is responsible for accomplishing his purposes
hrough the church.*

The fact that I serve God's church, for which he is ultimately responsible, releases me to deal freely with the people he entrusts into my care. Since God desires the "success" of my group much more than I do, and since he loves the members of my group much more, I am free to be his shepherd and steward. Let me illustrate.

As a young pastor and small-group leader, I was like the man in the parable of the talents who buried his talent because he was afraid (see Matthew 25). I too believed that God was harsh and demanding. I expected him to punish me if I did not produce. Hence, I tried doing everything myself or, at least, to have my hand in everything. Of course, the fear and control I modeled is what I reaped.

As God began healing my heart and renewing my mind in conformity to his, I started to let go and allow others to learn and make mistakes. This tough, even tortuous, season of my life has made all the difference in my ministry. Others grew in their leadership abilities as I released my grip on church ministries and the small group under my charge. I found many gifted, experienced, and teachable people who were more than ready to share responsibility for the church or small group.

When I say that God has more of a vested interest than we do in the success of our churches and small groups, I picture a caring and generous God preparing a bride worthy to be his. "Let us rejoice and be glad and give him glory! For the wedding of the Lamb has come, and his bride has made herself ready" (Revelation 19:7).

Trusting God to have our welfare always in mind, we believe furthermore that he will do whatever needs to be done to fulfill his plan, "even immeasurably more than all we ask or imagine, according to his power that is at work within us" (Ephesians 3:20). This includes people God has selected and gifted for service and ministry. Our job then is simple: find these people, recruit them, invest in them, and send them into appropriate places of service.

I wasn't always convinced of this. After years of struggling to fill slots, I once grew tired and fed up with the whole process. I was having no more success recruiting and keeping people productive in leadership positions than were my counterparts in business. In fact, many of my secular colleagues were having a much easier time of it than I. But after praying to God for months, I received some clues about my need for an attitude adjustment.

One clue came to me at a leadership forum in 1990 attended by representatives of mega-churches with extensive small-group ministries. Conference speaker Carl George said, "God has sent your church enough leaders to adequately care for all those in attendance. . . . He has even selected two out of every ten people in your church to lead."

Those statements troubled my soul for months. I stayed troubled until, in frustration, I committed to pray about them for direction and clarity.

I found a second clue in Jesus' statement, "For I did not speak of my own accord, but the Father who sent me commanded me what to say and how to say it. . . . But the world must learn that I love the Father and that I do exactly what my Father has commanded me" (John 12:49, 14:31).

I quickly realized that I had very little understanding of how our Father was calling and recruiting leaders to his church. So I began to pray, "Father, open my eyes to see and ears to hear, so I can hear and see who you are selecting." This was no big act of faith; I had had limited success with my own methods of leadership selection and development.

After praying this way for months, I began to see people differently. No longer did I look for only the good-looking, bright, successful business leaders. Rather, I looked for traits like faithfulness, integrity, servanthood, and a teachable spirit.

As I attune myself to God's Spirit through prayer and meditation on his Word, I choose to put aside my pre-conceived ideas of who will be a leader and who will not. My success rate of picking apprentices and potential leaders has risen incredibly.

I have spoken with pastors who fully expect problems if they train lay people to serve and lead. Some even fear losing their churches. This can be a self-fulfilling prophecy, since people do reap what they sow. If we sow fear, manipulation, and lack of trust, then our people will be tentative about receiving responsibility and commensurate authority. The fruit of their labors will be likely to spoil.

On the other hand, trust begets trust. People of all ages who are entrusted with increasing responsibility and given enough encouragement, will discover the reward of a job well done.

Assumption 2: I am an adult, and the people in my group are adults, so I can trust them to make adult decisions.

Years ago, when our toddler daughters, Molly and Stephanie, were first developing their mobility, my wife Chris and I helped them to establish safe boundaries. Portable fences at the top of the stairs and in doorways blocked access to hidden dangers. At times they resented the blockade, but we assured them it was for their own good—to keep them from touching a hot stove or tumbling down the stairs. Eventually, as they matured in their understanding and control of their bodies, we lowered and then removed the fences to allow them limited access to what was previously off-limits. I remember watching, with some trepidation, those first days of total freedom, as they explored areas formerly that were out of reach.

The objective with toddlers is "to time it right," that is, to expand the freedoms we give our children so that those freedoms coincide with their abilities. If we had not recognized

Molly's mental, physical, and emotional development and ha
kept the fences in place, she would have been limited (even
stunted) in her growth. Had we thrown open the whole hous
with little regard to Stephanie's safety, she would have most
likely been exposed to grave dangers.

As our daughters continued to mature, our parenting sty
had to keep changing. When they began new ventures on
their own—to join a slumber party, for example—we found i
healthy to point out what dangers might exist and the best o
the many choices available. Then we waited. When our
daughter returned home from whatever new venture it was,
we'd casually ask (hiding our real fears) how things went an
what she experienced. Occasionally, she'd choose to disregar
our counsel or warnings, and suffer the natural consequences. As much as we were tempted to protect her from
those consequences, we restrained ourselves. The consequences of their good and bad decisions have helped to mold
our daughters into the young ladies they have become.

Now that Molly and Stephanie are in senior high and
middle school, respectively, we are confronted once again wit
the need to adjust our parenting style. Going out with guys in
a church youth group or school club is no longer a trust issue
They have shown an ability to make good decisions regarding
their physical, spiritual, and emotional health. We are treatin
them more and more like young adults who need to plan,
make choices, and live with the results.

In the same way, as small-group leaders we may need to
adjust our leadership style as we go along. Even group member
who are young in Christ should be treated as adults who can
plan, make decisions, and live with results.

Check-Up Quiz

Does your leadership style need "an adjustment"?

To find out, give yourself this brief check-up quiz:

1. Do I speak to others under my leadership with respect,
   adult-to-adult?

2. Do I expect them not only to do the task or participate in the group, but to make important contributions that benefit everyone else?

3. Do I release others with room to do their job as they see fit?

4. Do I keep my opinion to myself, unless it is asked for?

To say that people in our churches need to be treated like adults may sound like I am belaboring the obvious. But I have seen pastoral leaders interact with subordinates and volunteer leaders as if they were talking to children. I've seen others spoken to as adults, but not given the authority to go along with their responsibilities. One such scene comes to mind. This pastoral leader was giving directions to a volunteer staff person who seemed like a wise, confident, and experienced lay leader in his own right. But his instructor treated him like a child, saying, "You need to . . . ," and "If you don't, . . . then I won't be able to let you do this again."

The implication for the recipient of this instruction was threefold: (1) the teacher's favor had to be curried; (2) her trust had to be earned; and (3) if the "student" did not match up to her expectations, he'd be denied additional opportunities to serve or lead. Over the long term, this behavior can cripple the lay leader with shame and guilt. This leadership style may then "trickle down" to other group leaders throughout church, affecting the whole lay ministry.

However, when church leaders trust God to give gifts to men and women, and equip them to "do the work of ministry" (Ephesians 4:11), the productivity, joy, and expectation of our fellow workers will greatly increase. When someone tells me they see great potential in me, invests some time and energy in me, and convinces me they're in it with me for the long haul, then there is no stopping me. That's when I feel like "I can do all things through him who gives me strength!" (Philippians 4:13).

Assumption 3: Change is scary, but I can handle it without having to control everything.

If I look at the health and size of my group as being limited by what I can accomplish, then it will only get as big or as healthy as what I can get my arms around. Obviously, this is a dangerous mindset. If, however, I adopt Assumption 3, the issue of control is resolved in healthy ways. Just as biological cells grow and reproduce themselves in our bodies, contributing to human health and growth, so also small groups that grow and reproduce fulfill God's design for church health and growth.

We are to maximize the potential of the people we train. That's a wonderful gift we give to them, and to God, for it reflects the very nature of our loving, caring Father in heaven. We shine the most when we stir up hope in those around us, hope that they can also participate in the plans and purposes of God here on earth.

Ashley Montagu, the great philanthropist, says that many people suffer from psychosclerosis, which is like arteriosclerosis or the "hardening of the arteries." Psychosclerosis is hardening of the attitudes. You may not need a heart transplant or an arterial graft, but you may have the early warning signs (or even an advanced case) of this dreaded disease. If you do, don't despair, for many sufferers of psychosclerosis have benefited from Jesus' healing touch.

Check-Up Quiz

Are you suffering from psychosclerosis?

We can participate in God's wondrous plan for healthy church growth by developing mentoring relationships with others in the group. To see if you are actually doing this, here's another check-up quiz:

1. Are you willing to invest in others to the point where their success or failure depends on the Holy Spirit, not on your ability to prop them up?

2. Do you invite potential leaders to experiment with their developing leadership style in the safe confines of your group, even when you'd rather do it yourself?

3. Are you training others to make difficult decisions and do problem-solving on their own, even if you think you have the answer?

Chapter 3

The Power of Planning, or "An Ounce of Prevention"

"I know God will not give me anything I can't handle. I just wish that he didn't trust me so much."
—**Mother Teresa**

"Few people think more than two or three times a year; I have made an international reputation for myself by thinking once or twice a week."
—**George Bernard Shaw**

My father worked as a maintenance superintendent for a large aluminum products company. Whenever a furnace broke down, this caused the whole production line to stall. So my father became a big advocate of preventive maintenance. He had standing orders for the maintenance managers and personnel to constantly oil the machinery, to schedule down-time for regular maintenance, to prevent at all costs work-stoppages due to breakdowns. Many unforeseeable problems still required my dad's presence in the plant. But he headed off many problems because he focused on prevention, not repair.

Avoid falling into the time trap

I have watched many in small-group leadership get caught in the time trap. That trap is sprung if we do not take simple pre-cautions, or proactive steps, to protect the time set aside to pre-pare for our group. "Things and stuff" will sidetrack us from the more excellent way. This time trap is often baited with:

► Procrastination tendencies—using any excuse to delay starting;
► Interruptions—some are ministry opportunities, but many are not;
► Unnecessary activities (reading all the mail, watching TV);
► Drop-in visits—again, some are good, some can be postponed.

Proactive small-group leaders set aside preparation time as sacred—a date with God, to seek his face and guidance. Expect the Holy Spirit to guide you into all truth—the truth about Scripture, but also the truth about your group members and what's best for them at this time. Remember, this does not have to be a struggle. Since God created you and your group, he knows exactly what it takes to convince you of his leading, if you ask and believe that he will.

Before I learned and applied this approach to my studies, I was a frequent victim of the time trap. I used to have these wonderful group lesson plans all formulated in my mind, and then someone would phone or drop by, asking if they could interrupt. Invariably I said "Yes," fearing that if I didn't, I'd miss out on something important or I'd offend that person. But in allowing interruptions, I was really saying, "I don't think this particular relationship can handle a 'No.'"

I've since grown confident in myself and in my relationships with others. Hence, I am much more comfortable with setting limits or boundaries on my relationships. I do this so I can maintain my relationship with God, my wife Chris, our children, and even have time for myself.

Boundaries, or space-and-time limits, are increasingly important to any leader, as demands on our time increase all around us. Realistically, we can only be best friends with a few people, good friends with a perhaps a few dozen, and acquaintances with many more.

Avoid losing "all your marbles"

I cannot allow anybody to make bigger demands on me than what I have the resources of time, energy, and compassion to offer. Here's an analogy that helps me understand this dynamic principle.

Each morning God hands me a bag of marbles—just enough marbles to get me through the day with sufficiency in all things. My spouse needs some marbles of attention and time, so she gets a few marbles off the top. My children need the same investment in them, so there go a few more marbles. I head off to work where my employees need marbles. One colleague in particular is going through a hard time and needs a few more. I dispense marbles to those who "do lunch," call, fax, and e-mail me throughout the day.

By the time I get home, my bag of marbles is getting close
to empty. One daughter shares her significant story of getting hurt that day, so I comfort her with a few marbles.
After dinner, at our small group, I hand out more marbles,
with one or two extra for those with special needs. At
home again I'm handed a note saying an acquaintance
called with an urgent plea for a return call—a note with
two exclamation points!!

Now I am at the bottom of my bag, with no marbles left
for myself or my relationship with my Father. How could
this happen? I go to bed, concluding that I've lost my
marbles.

Sound familiar? In his perfect plan, the eternal God of all
creation had either miscalculated and was caught by
surprise, or I had given away more marbles than he had
provided. I conclude that somewhere I gave out marbles to
people and things that God had not intended.

Until I come to see the problem as my own, and take
appropriate steps "not to lose all my marbles," I will always be
in a deficit mode, borrowing marbles on credit ("I'll make it up
to you tomorrow, I promise."). That credit line wears thin, as
tomorrow comes and goes with no deposit of time and emotional energy, only another withdrawal of marbles. Suddenly,
you are in bankruptcy court.

Marbles are like manna, God's provision for today, which we
cannot hoard or receive on credit. God's provision—of marbles
or manna—is to be managed for God and given away with joy.
We recognize our limits when we say, "I don't know; I'm sorry, I
cannot help you." We set boundaries and offer help when we
say, "I do not have the resources to help you now, but I can point
you to another who may." (Or, "I'll dig out the answer and come
back to you at a later time.")

Boundaries prevent us from giving away life-resources that
are meant to keep us balanced and healthy. While methods of
boundary-setting and small-group preparation vary, good leaders use their devotional time to seek a fresh encounter with
God. This time together also replenishes one's marbles or
manna daily, out of which the leader then has something to
share with others and lead small groups.

"Work your plan" and "Plan by values"

Having planned your work, it's time to work your plan. For me that means I plan by my values, not by time, circumstances, or goals. These values flow out of a personal vision (of what you want to accomplish with your life) and a mission statement (which translates that vision into a practical strategy of measurable steps or action plans). A personal vision and mission statement are born out of much thought and prayer over a period of time. The result of this process is energizing. I come away with renewed direction, a reconfirmed calling, and the commitment to see it through.

Values can be simply defined as "whatever you willingly put your time, money, and energy into," that is, your priorities, preferences, and practices. Practices are activities that you do on a regular or priority basis and express your values. These values will be evident, for example, to anyone with access to your weekly planner or checkbook.

There are life or family values, and there are work values. To see how this theory works out in practice, let's take, for example, my own work arena, the Pilgrimage Training Group, where I put my values into practice.

- ☑ My **personal vision** for Pilgrimage is "To empower and encourage the Church throughout North America to value and pursue a deeper level of Christian community in obedience to the Great Commandment."
- ☑ Our **mission** is to accomplish this by: (1) offering interactive training seminars led by a team of pastors who teach and train from their own practical experience, and (2) publishing study guides, books, and tapes that help leaders build significant Christian community.
- ☑ The **values** that flow from my vision and mission are active involvement in a small-group ministry, recruiting, teaching, modeling, and encouraging others.
- ☑ My calendar-at-a-glance reveals established **practices** that show how I live out my values. There's a scheduled weekly small group. There are regular monthly sessions where I oversee a handful of small groups in my home church. My checkbook shows I'm constantly spending money to train people for small-group leadership locally, as well as nationally and internationally.

All who call themselves disciples of Jesus are "called" into his service in some way or other, so I look for people who are not presently serving or leading—people whom I then invite into the process in low-risk, fun ways. I draw them into ministries of service or leadership by briefing them about what we are going to do, modeling the action or task to be done (by doing this myself, whenever possible), and then debriefing after we are done.

rief-Model-Debrief

This simple method lowers the overall threshold of anxiety so that these folks can get on board. The "debriefing" process allows them to ask, "Why did you do that?" or "Why did you say that?" This allows me to show how simple or natural "doing church" is supposed to be. By inviting others along, I ease them into some area of service or leadership almost before they know it, and they don't feel pulled or pushed in the process.

Suppose I want to use this method to introduce someone to the important small-group leader task of developing and living by a personal mission statement. Since I cannot lead others where I'm not willing to go, I share my experience in this area. For example, I might talk about the value of a mountain getaway to develop my personal mission statement.

A few years ago, a close friend of mine was counseling me in response to concerns about my direction in life. I shared that I had many doubts, fears, and frustrations because of some major decisions that I had made the previous year. After sharing with me some valuable insights from his own life and difficulties he had worked through, he said, "You need to go to the mountains (I live outside Denver) and spend some time with God. Don't come down till he gives you the answers you need."

I had a hard time in those mountains. I went with a friend who was also examining big issues in his life. We spent periods of time alone (with no TV, radio, or telephone), then got together to talk and debrief. The results were powerful. Spending 48 hours in that setting turned our time of prayer and whining to God into a time of listening within the silence to God's revelation and direction.

What I learned was more than I had bargained for. I learned that I do not take time to listen to God. Yet I know the value of spending time with my Father who loves me. How could that be? I wonder to myself.

Down in the valley where I live day-to-day, I still need to set aside various times to seek him out—a moment here, a moment there, a few hours over here, an occasional day over there. I find this practice of renewing my vision genuinely enriches my understanding of who I am, what I should invest my life in, and broadens my understanding of how to train, lead, and affect others through small groups. Those times almost always remind me to invest my time, energy, and money in the things I truly value.

Self-examination and accountability

Any honest assessment of where you are investing or spending your life will involve a look at your checkbook or credit card statement, as well as your daily planner and your work and family calendars.

If you do not use a planner, it is a simple discipline to begin. Purchase one that fits you, one that you can keep with you most of the time. This tool allows you to budget your time, just as a written financial budget allows you to plan where and when you will spend your money.

With your planner, sit down at least once a week and make your first appointments with family members, with others, and time just for yourself. This "time for self" allows one to regularly meet God in his Word, in prayer, to grow through professional and recreational reading, and to enjoy physical exercise.

By planning your time according to your values and priorities, you will also begin to see a difference in how you plan and prepare for small group, as well as in your relationships with group members. When a member contacts me and asks for some time, I look in my planner to see if I have the requested time available. If it falls within a time frame I have set apart for myself, I can simply say, "Sorry, I already have an appointment during that time. Would this other time work?"

Resist the temptation to regard your personal time as the most flexible or replaceable of your appointments. Giving in at that point will leave you short of your goals and will prevent you from growing. If you do not make appointments with yourself, you will live by the "tyranny of the urgent," always allowing other things and circumstances to dictate your schedule, sap your energy, and steal your marbles.

Planning is, of course, more than a good preventative maintenance program for your small-group life. If used regularly, planning with your values in mind can simplify and energize your life. Planning undoes the damage of wasting your life-resources as you bounce from crisis to crisis.

Ask yourself the hard questions to determine why you are not attending to those priorities. Invite another trusted person to help you examine your schedule or your checkbook. More often than not, your accountability partner will bring greater objectivity to this task of self-examination. Spend some time with God and ask him to direct your steps and to establish your plans. He will, if you will ask!

Check-Up Quiz

Do you have healthy boundaries?

Take a few minutes today and examine where you are investing your life-resources. A check-up quiz will help you see if you are building healthy boundaries that preserve your preparation time for small group. This will, in turn, increase the productivity of your small group.

1. Is there anyone who regularly demands more from me than is healthful? (How can I respond to those individuals so that, when finished, I will not feel drained or like I'm in a deficit situation?)

2. What self-imposed limits will help me choose activities, meetings, recreation, and the like? (How can I be accountable in this process?)

3. What volunteer activity is unhealthy for me, pushing me outside of my comfort zone, or robbing me of relationship time with God, family and self that I so desperately need? (What steps can I take to move toward balance and health?)

4. Where can I spend time alone to prepare for my group that will maximize the opportunity and minimize distractions? (Is there a place at home, work, school, or public library that provides this?)

5. What will I need to complete my study time and make it most productive? (Any resource materials or printed curriculum? Any instructions for the leader? Any Bible study to prepare from scratch?)

6. Do I need to begin working on a series of related lessons? (Would it make sense to outline the whole series, so I can keep some continuity?)

7. Am I accomplishing what God has placed in my heart to do?

Chapter 4

Using Creativity to Trouble-Shoot Small-Group Problems Before They Break Out

*"Creativity can solve almost any problem.
The creative act, the defeat of habit by originality,
overcomes everything."*
—George Lois

*"Creativity represents a miraculous coming together
of the uninhibited energy of the child with its apparent
opposite and enemy, the sense of order imposed
on the disciplined adult intelligence."*
—Norman Podhoretz

"Whether you think you can or can't, you're right."
—Henry Ford

*"Why does man have creativity? Why can man think of many
things in his mind and choose, and then bring forth something
that other people can taste, smell, hear, feel and see? Because
man was created in the image of a Creator. Man was created
that he might create.*
—Edith Schaeffer

We all know people whom we call "creative-types" or "risk-takers." Some are off-the-wall crazy, even reckless thrill-seekers—not the kind we'd want driving our daughter to the prom. But there's a perfectly healthy and reasonable brand of creativity and risk-taking that I want to incorporate into my personal and small-group life. Creative risk will make the difference between a lifeless group and a life-giving group.

Creativity is vital to the process of trouble-shooting in small groups. I believe creativity is latent within everyone and the Holy Spirit can stir it up. Unless we know how to bring out and work with the creativity in others, we cannot help them overcome the barriers to the fulfillment of their goals.

The need for creativity in small-group ministry

Creativity is expressed in an almost infinite variety of ways, but supremely through God in Christ. God's creativity was expressed in and through everything that Jesus said and did. Jesus was active from the beginning of Creation (John 1:1-3) and throughout his life (turning water into wine, feeding the 5,000, healing the sick).

On one of his last days on earth, Jesus the carpenter told professional fisherman where to find a boatload of fish. They knew perfectly well how to fish, where to fish, and when to fish (John 21:1-14). Here was Jesus, appearing to them in a newly resurrected body, asking them to do things they had never tried before. Only by obedience—by risking more failure and humiliation—would they receive the blessing of taking a risk for Jesus.

Does your walk with God feel repetitious, too comfortable, even listless, like a well-worn shoe? Even the good things in our lives can become lifeless when we don't do them with purpose, with the mind of Christ.

Stepping out of one's comfort zone, discarding all excuses and crutches ("but-we've-never-done-it-that-way-before")—that's what the paralytic by the pool of Bethesda had to do (John 5:2–6). Only then could he get well. An invalid for 38 years, this man was full of excuses and content with the status quo, or so it would seem, until Jesus asked him, "Do you want to get well?"

Jesus always pushes past our surface condition and the roadblocks we put up. He goes for the heart. Likewise, a good small-group leader is never content with an obvious "Yes," or "Fine, thank you," or "The answer is A." The Christlike or creative leader will disturb the waters and stir up convictions about truth, heartfelt desire, and creative alternatives.

The question Jesus asked the paralytic by the pool is being asked of us, "Are you willing to lay aside your history, to stop seeing yourself through the sickness and sins of your past, to step outside your present comfort zone, and take on a new view of yourself and your future?"

Learning is change

In Christian ministry, leaders wrestle with the clash of two cultures every day: The Unchanging Word and The Constantly Changing World. Alvin Toffler (author of *Future Shock*) predicts who will survive that clash: "The illiterate of the year 2000 will not be the individual who cannot read and write, but the one who cannot learn, unlearn and relearn."[1]

John Naisbitt (author of *Megatrends*) makes a similar point about learning: "In the new information society where the only constant is change, we can no longer expect to get an education and to be done with it. There is no one education, no one skill, that lasts a lifetime now. Like it or not, the information society has turned all of us into life-long learners."[2]

This attitude of being lifelong learners influences how we see Scripture and know God. Our calling as small-group leaders is also one of lifelong learning. Accepting change is how we'll reach future generations and cultural groups around us. The Bible gives us our values and functions, which don't change with the times.

For example, the functions of evangelism, service, discipleship, fellowship, and worship will always be the Church's calling. However, the *forms* and *delivery* of these functions must change with each generation and cultural group. That means small groups allow for, even require, different approaches for different people.

Creative change leads to spiritual renewal

When my church in Cincinnati was poised for growth, we needed to find a new form to deliver the ageless truth of the gospel. With our traditional approach to evangelism, we saw fewer and fewer results. At one particular staff meeting, we noticed rerouted traffic backing up for a mile outside our church property because of a summer-long highway construction project on the beltline. We had all experienced the tempers flaring, the delays, and frustration over the previous weeks. Our church administrator (Jim) then had a stroke of creative insight: "Let's do something tangible to relieve the tension of those stuck in the traffic."

In a brainstorming session, our small group of pastors decided to give out cold drinks in Jesus' name (Mark 9:41) to the people caught in those interminable traffic delays. Jobs were assigned, teams were formed, signs were made ("Free Drinks Ahead"), coolers were filled, carts were wheeled into place.

Under the pop-top of each can, we slid a church business card—with all the basic information, plus this statement:

*You looked too thirsty to pass up! We hope this small gif.
brings some light into your day. It's a simple way of saying
God loves you—no strings attached. Let us know if we can be
of more assistance.*

We worked both sides of the street, operating from card
tables. Each pastor on call handed out hundreds of cans from
4:30–5:30 P.M. that first Friday!

You should have seen the appreciative looks on the drivers' faces as they were touched by a simple act of kindness.
That was rewarding enough, but many of those people came
to "check out" a church that hands out free drinks on the
roadside.

My point in retelling the story here is not to focus on the
acts of kindness or the fruit of our labors, but on how we
brainstormed for creative solutions and seized the moment
God had given us. We changed our ways and learned that
"working both sides of the street" can be Christian. We were
creative because Jesus called us to imitate him in being creative in our evangelism.

As we shared this "preachers-in-the-street" and "can-of-
pop-in-Jesus'-name" story with our church members, it
caught fire. The excitement level grew. Small groups began to
discuss how to meet the needs of the people living in the
neighborhoods. This proved infectious and it multiplied.

Soon simple acts of unsolicited kindness became the
norm.[3] Thousands of people were touched through group
service projects. Hundreds came to the groups and to the
church to see why we'd concern ourselves with the little
needs of the average person. By thinking creatively, we won a
hearing for the gospel! Many who heard the gospel stayed.

What is "creative thinking" and how do I do it?

Creative thinking can be simply and variously stated: "allowing yourself to look at a familiar problem in a different
way" . . . "stepping out of your pew into the marketplace of
ideas" . . . "combing through your experiences for parable-
like stories to tell" . . . "breaking the rules" . . . "throwing
away the molds" . . . "looking for strange bedfellows to partner with." In sum, creative thinking in small-group ministry
requires that we open up our thinking process to new possibilities and to change.

To facilitate church health and growth, do not allow all the creative ideas to come from you. Besides, making every decision for the groups from the top down is a trap. Encourage group members to participate in all planning stages and to help create all group functions. Small groups of all kinds become shallow and stale when limited to one person's perspective on life.

Inviting people to work through seemingly small situations together allows them to develop confidence in resolving those real crisis situations down the road. We in the Western world demand that paid staff in our churches do the hard work or make all the hard decisions. This attitude trickles down to volunteer small-group leaders, as well. But it is fallacious and burdensome to think that professional leaders have a bottomless well of creativity, knowledge, or compassion.

The top-down, one-leader-does-it-all model is also unbiblical. God distributed spiritual gifts for "some to be apostles . . . prophets . . . evangelists . . . pastors and teachers to prepare God's people for works of service, so that the body of Christ may be built up" (Ephesians 4:11–13).

This all-in-it-together attitude is healthy and edifying. When this attitude grabs the entire church, the incredible power of the laity is unleashed. When people in the pew begin to pray, when people looking for opportunity to serve actually put their hand to the plow, when people who enjoy member "privileges" begin to take group "ownership" and "duties" seriously—watch out! Here comes the Church!

This creative group process is encouraged by an atmosphere where people can share their offbeat or incomplete ideas. With an accepting demeanor, press for different views or applications of Scripture. State your expectations up front: "There are no wrong answers in this exercise," or "The only bad idea is the one you don't share!"

You can also draw group members into creative thinking by using simple exercises designed to enhance creative solutions. Try this one:

Can you think of a way in which you put a sheet of newspaper on the floor so that when two people stand face to face on it, they won't be able to touch one another? Cutting or tearing the paper is not allowed. Neither is tying the two people up to prevent them from moving.[4]

Jesus Christ, the supreme change agent

With creativity comes surprise! Jesus majored in the unexpected, doing things that caught people off guard and pushing his disciples to look at life from another angle:

► Jesus went not to the high and mighty, but to the demon-possessed, the reviled, the outcast (Luke 8).
► The Jews expected their Messiah to break the oppressive Roman rule, but Jesus instructed them to carry the soldier's gear two miles instead of one (Matthew 5:41).
► Jesus commanded people to turn the other cheek, to lend without expecting a return, to love their enemies (Luke 6:29,34–35).
► Jesus turned Lazarus' funeral into a party that celebrated the resurrection (John 11).
► Jesus dined in the home of a hated tax collector (Luke 19:7).
► Jesus went against Jewish law by healing on the Sabbath.
► Jesus fed the 5,000 after first saying to his disciples, "Where shall we buy bread for these people to eat?" (John 6:5).
► Instead of ushering in the Kingdom with a sword, Jesus chose a cross.

Look out for "brain blockades"

Why don't we think more creatively more often? There are several possible reasons. The biggest is fear, but two others stand out. First, we don't need to be creative for most of our daily functions (showering, changing clothes, commuting to work), so we get used to functioning on autopilot. Second, we haven't been taught creativity by our educational system. Rather, we learn rote memorization, and we try to guess what the teacher is thinking. (Do you recall any teachers asking, "What original ideas do you have?" or "In what other ways can you respond to this information?")

Hence, we develop attitudes that lock our thinking into the status quo and keep us from being creative. I call these attitudes "brain blockades." To overcome brain blockades and cut through status quo thinking, we need the approach of physicist Tom Hirshfield, who said, "The second assault on the same problem should come from a totally different direction."

My former colleague, Steve Sjogren, was good at this. Steve always pushed me to look at any problem from a variety of angles, even some ways I felt were risky, or out of my comfort zone. Once, when our recovery group ministry was ready to reach out to people in our community who struggled with addictions and compulsions, Steve came up with a strange, highly provocative, yet most productive idea.

He noted the lifestyle of many people in recovery meetings around the city: They smoked cigarettes, and many chain-smoked. So Steve ordered thousands of packs of matches with our church logo on the front, a catchy phrase on the back, with a map and information inside the matchbook. Volunteers from our own church-based recovery groups made the rounds of all the other "recovery houses" in the city and left cartons of these matchbooks. Bars and taverns were not exempt, either, from this outreach.

These matchbooks worked better than many tracts we had passed out. Smokers saw our church's invitation for days at a time, each time they lit up!

Some of our members criticized us for encouraging smoking. But people who already smoke perceive their need for matches, not lectures. By Steve's willingness to look at life from their perspective, we served a felt need and gave them an invitation to church. In the process, we broke through a "brain blockade."

We can all learn from the creativity of successful leaders. But God has even more to teach us about creative thinking if we will learn from our failures:

► What are the three biggest mistakes you made in the past five years?

► Look at one of these failures for the silver lining. What were the beneficial consequences to you? To your spouse? To your family?

Looking at failure through this "lens" may help you overcome barriers and develop new facets of your leadership. You can even learn to see some benefit in the resistance that group members exhibit when they are confronted with change.

arning to deal with resistance

A friend of mine and his wife had to learn the hard way when snorkeling in the Gulf of Mexico. A good distance from shore, after inspecting all the coral reef and gorgeous tropical fish that lived there, they turned to swim back. They swam and swam in a direct line but made no headway and were soon exhausted. No one had told them of the rip tide, which was much stronger than they were. Finally, it dawned on them to swim at a diagonal to the shoreline, using some of the powerful tidal action of the gulf waters to help them reach the shore

It's tough to get anywhere when you go against the current. Unique ideas are always resisted. ("What is this going to cost me?" "What am I going to have to give up?" "I love change—as long as it happens to someone else.") This reality can be as difficult as swimming upstream.

This does not mean you should give up. That spells death. Group leaders who take risks will make headway if they go "diagonally" with the flow. If you believe in your idea, go for it. Take steps to introduce change slowly and invite others into the process. But know that there will be resistance.

Overcoming a change agent's worst enemy—fear

Fear is one of the biggest barriers to creativity. It locks up the mind and won't let it function. But fear is also a sign of a creative mind. Fear shows the power of the imagination. The problem with fear is that creativity is turned the wrong way, producing worries instead of solutions.

Fear is hard to deal with because it is based on misunderstanding or ignorance, and is masked as anger, frustration, apologies, or excuses. In order to help others overcome fear of change, you must take the time to understand what they are afraid of and why.

A while back, the members of a small group I led were delivering bags of groceries from our church's food pantry to the sick, the poor, and the shut-ins across town. One couple in our group had a panicked look on their faces and began spouting feeble apologies and excuses. Since we never demand that anyone do anything in ministry they are not comfortable with, I backed off. But their unease was so out of character for them that I felt a need to press further.

I then learned they had both grown up in a small segregated town full of racial bigotry and feared for their lives if they went to that part of town! I assured them that teams of people from the church went to those parts of town almost weekly, and we hadn't lost anyone yet. But it took months of testimonies from group members before they could or would hear the truth. Eventually, we removed a fear that was rooted in generations of ignorance and bias.

However, we may unnecessarily put people at risk if our idea is not carefully thought through. In that case, we are our own worst enemy. If you hold your idea too close to the vest, without opening yourself up to criticism, you may fail to see its weaknesses.

Now it's your own fear that you must overcome. Find someone you can share your ideas with who won't shoot you down, but will be honest with you! You don't want a "yes man." (Where two always agree, one is not necessary.) What you need is a person who can be objective and tell you the truth in love. That someone, in my case, is most often my wife Chris. As a different personality type, she easily sees holes in my ideas or difficulties that I overlooked. Chris knows how to give feedback in ways I can receive it best.

sing opposition to gain new insights

The creative process is often a dynamic oscillation between opposites. To understand the positive or upside, we must know the negative or downside. We all are blind to problems that arise in our own thinking, so God brings opposites together to help us see better. An opposing view can point out my blind-side or keep me from rushing into disaster.

When we know how opposites interact, we often have the solution to our problem. A case in point is the time when a young church in an unfamiliar community across the state invited me to move. Because that church could really benefit from my background and expertise, I considered the call. After considerable prayer, Chris and I concluded that was God's will for us.

However, I had also asked my close friend, another pastor, to pray with me over a period of time and counsel me. When I told him about this decision to take the call, he replied, "Thom, I believe you misunderstood God's intent on this matter. I feel that if you move, it will be a huge mistake."

Now I was stunned. His input made me double-check myself and wait. This allowed me some time to be even more objective, and to allow God to sort out faith from presumption. In the end, I took the position in the new church. Our service there turned out to be an incredibly productive and fruitful time of ministry!

My point? Listen to the counsel of your detractors. Develop a "thick skin" if need be, but listen. Then sift the "wheat from the chaff"—that is, the truth to receive and act upon, and the parts to disregard.

God allows adversity to come upon us to strengthen us! "My grace is sufficient for you, for my power is made perfect in weakness" (2 Corinthians 12:9). The apostle Paul grasped the truth that God uses our weakness and adverse circumstances to prove his power, provision, and protection.

Check-Up Quiz

How to flex your "risk muscle"

Consider a recent situation or a current relationship you are struggling with regarding your small-group ministry. These questions, which will serve as a helpful pop quiz and review of this chapter, will also help you work through your doubts or dreams concerning creative ministry options:

1. If you could do anything, what would enable you to accomplish your greatest dreams in this area of ministry?

2. What huge risk (or step of faith) could you take today that would revolutionize your approach to this ministry?

3. What is the most you could lose by taking these risks?

4. What might you gain?

Learning to exercise and flex your "risk muscle" may, at first, be hard work, like going to the club to work out when you haven't done a thing for months. But as in toning your body, flexing this muscle will affect every area of your life in a positive way!

---

[1]Alvin Toffler, *Future Shock* (New York: Bantam, 1991), page 36.

[2]John Naisbitt, *Megatrends: Ten New Directions Transforming Our Live* (New York: Warner, 1984), page 92.

[3]For more information on what has been termed "Servant Evangelism," see Steve Sjogren, *Conspiracy of Kindness* (Ann Arbor: Servant Publications, 1993).

[4]Try putting the paper in a closed doorway with one person on either side.

Chapter 5

Do You Govern by
Policies or Principles?

"Saddle your dreams afore you ride 'em."
—Mary Webb

"Every rule here can be challenged except this one."
—A sign on the wall of a young inventive corporation

*"Again no regrets. Don't look at the past and say,
'What a waste.' Make it a rule of life never to regret and never
look back. Regret is an appalling waste of energy; you can't
build on it; it's only good for wallowing in."*
—Katherine Mansfield

There is a side in all of us that tends toward legalism. When we
do not know how to respond, or do not want to invest the
required energy to respond in compassion and grace, it is easier to make a rule. When challenged by something or someone
we don't understand, we tend to invent and impose a rule to
force compliance.

Policies can squelch creativity

My daughter Stephanie is a case in point. She is very creative
and tends to see life differently than do many of her fellow students and even her parents. When she was four or five years of
age, she expressed her creative side through the clothes she
chose to wear. We controlled what she had to choose from, as
we purchased her clothing. But she had total control over what
combinations she made out of her little wardrobe.

Sometimes I cringed at the colors and patterns she
"matched" up. Often she wore two pairs of contrasting
socks—pink on one foot, green on another. Most days she
quickly tired of these artistic statements and changed her
entire outfit five or six times in a day! Now in school, she
excels in classes where she is allowed to express her creativity, but tends to struggle in classes that demand a regimen.

Her grades usually reflect this disparity, as well. I struggle
with teachers who demand that she do her work according to

their rules and assumptions. Obviously, Stephanie needs to learn that there are norms for living that she needs to accept. But I am afraid that she may have that wonderful creative side snuffed out by the policies and rules of teachers who don't necessarily relate to her "right-brained" approach to life. I also recognize that we need a grading system to determine the progress of students who are willing to make mistakes and venture outside the lines. As we become accustomed to the policy of penalizing mistakes, we restrict our natural urge to investigate alternate answers or approaches to solving problems.

Much of our educational system, and consequently our churches, consists of dispensing information, then testing to see if the high school student or Bible student can give it back in the "right" order. Math tables and spelling, for example, force students to memorize foundational precepts. But Albert Einstein and many other creative people were labeled "idiots" or "unteachable" because they did not fit this norm of fact-gathering. Creative types have a different way of knowing and understanding. We educators—and small-group leaders—should find ways to accommodate this non-traditional way of learning.

"Standing Orders"—obey the Word

I am frequently confronted by people who complain they are not getting enough "meat" in the teaching portion of their particular small group. Or they want to start more content-loaded Bible studies themselves. I agree with this perceived need to be in the Word of God more than we are. But I usually answer such complaints with this question, "Of all the Bible information or spiritual knowledge you have acquired, how much would you say you are currently using to help the lost, the sick, the poor, the lonely, or simply to live out the Great Commandment and Great Commission?" In other words, for everyone who wants more small groups that emphasize knowing and interpreting the Word, I want small groups who are obeying and doing it.

Every soldier has "standing orders" which are memorized for instant recall and automatic implementation. Standing orders are the "default mode," so to speak, that every soldier falls back on. By extension, I believe that the Great Commandment ("to love God and neighbor," Matthew

22:36–40) and the Great Commission ("to make disciples of every nation"—Matthew 28:18–20) are the default mode, or standing orders that all soldiers of Christ live by.

A policy is meant to point out a clear direction and to help establish limits for us. But if a policy no longer guides the group toward fulfilling its goals and mission and has become more of a stumbling block, then keep the principle, but that policy has got to go.

"Policies will change, principles never do."

Most of the rules we live by are unwritten traditions. They have been passed down and adopted by group consent. I am reminded of the story of four generations of women who prepared ham for their holiday together:

> The two youngest, a young mother and daughter, were in the kitchen preparing the ham roast. As the young girl observed the way her mother prepared ham, she inquired, "Why do you cut off the end of the ham?"
>
> The young mother replied, "That is just the way your grandmother taught me. Why don't you go ask her?"
>
> The young girl approached her grandmother with the same question, "Why do you cut off the end of the ham?"
>
> The grandmother answered, "Well, that is just the way your great-grandmother taught me. Why don't you go ask her?"
>
> So she did. And great-grandma's response was, "When I was a young girl learning how to cook, we only had a small pan, so we always cut off the end of the ham."

The unwritten rules or traditions of small groups also carry great power! Tradition can develop in virtually no time at all, never mind four generations of mothers' recipes.

A classic example of this took place in a group I once led, where the expectations and assumptions about starting "on time" were called into question by those with a longstanding policy of showing up late. I started the group with three or four others, feeling confident we were all on the same page. The starting time for the group was 7:00 P.M. Within weeks, a handful of group members began strolling in ten minutes late. Because the dynamics were different without them, I began to delay the start of the group, explaining to those who showed up on time that I did not want to repeat any important material. Finally, a woman spoke up the third time I delayed the meeting, "Why are you penalizing those of us who make the effort to arrive on time? By holding up the meeting, you are only encouraging the misbehavior of those who are continually late."

She had a point. After I recovered from my embarrassment, I thanked her for the mid-course correction and decided to begin the group thereafter at the appointed hour regardless of who was on hand. Most people got the message. One or two will never be on time, but I haven't knowingly encouraged this behavior, or lack of group discipline, again.

In making rules or policies, a good rule of thumb in examining them is, "Is this policy going to help others grow and excel, or is it intended to control and limit? I like what John Maxwell wrote in this regard,

Policies are many,
Principles are few,
Policies will change,
Principles never do.

A principle is a high standard we attempt to achieve in everyday life. Some examples of principles I live by: "Always tell the truth the first time"; "Don't export what you don't live"; "Whenever possible, err on the side of mercy"; and "To bring out the best in others, catch them doing something right and praise them for it."

These principles and those spelled out in this book (on time management, preventive maintenance, etc.) govern my life more than rules and regulations. If I am to teach principles to my children and to those I lead, I must model them. Some principles are better "caught" than "taught." If we give our attention to principles to live by, we'll spend much less time and energy worrying about rules or policies.

Be open to those who challenge your rules and policies. If no one challenges your rules of operation, or if you squelch sincere objections to the usual *modus operandi*, this can lead small groups into dangerous waters. First, we could get locked into a single approach, strategy, or method without seeing that there are other more appropriate ways of doing small-group business.

Secondly, we could fall into blind allegiance to a method or rule that no longer works or makes sense. This second danger is the point of the ham-cut-in-half-to-fit-the-oven-pan story. In small groups (as in the four generations of women who prepared the ham roast) we make rules based on what we observe other reasonable people doing. We then follow these rules and pass them on to others, often for generations. As time passes, circumstances behind the original reason for the rules change, yet the rules stay in place. The original reason for cutting off the back half of the ham no longer exists (we now have a larger oven or a bigger baking dish than our grandmother), but because the rules are still in place, we continue to throw away perfectly good food.

mall-group rules and models to reexamine

Rules in small groups may include the order of the meeting. But who says the order has to be the same each time? Why not change the order to place more emphasis on one aspect of the meeting? Why not set aside the group agenda when someone comes into the room hurting and needs special attention?

Rules can also dictate the focus and the type of people my group affects. While direction and a covenant are important, I believe groups, like people, grow through seasons and cycles. We need to adjust our leadership style accordingly and go with the flow.

From a church-wide perspective I learned an important lesson about leading a small group. The lesson came a few years ago when our church examined the actual numbers of people who regularly attended a small group. While the numbers seemed impressive, they fell far short of our goals. We spent considerable time examining various avenues we had already tried to encourage our church members to join a group. At one of these meetings, we asked, "Is the type of group we are doing limiting the participation of our people?"

It was a hard question, because we had refined and honed this model over a few years, and it worked for those who were attracted to it. Perhaps more than one model was in order. So the discussion encompassed a wide range of other models.

Our basic group model was integrated by age, gender, and marital status, geared to fellowship, application-type Bible study, and "one-another" ministry. It doesn't get any better than that, right?

Wrong. In interviews with dozens of people not in groups, I heard some real eye-opening tales. I heard the usual excuses ("not enough time," "no child care at the group," and "we already have enough friends"). But I also heard something I should have suspected—that groups were a scary proposition! No matter how hard I tried to dissuade people from their unreasonable fears, this response was strong.

I also heard from people who wanted more concentrated Bible study, a group just for women, or a support group dealing with seasonal life-and-loss issues such as new parents, or empty nesters. Now we had some concrete information to work with.

Over the next two years, we developed a system of eight different types of groups. Some met as seldom as once a month, geared to making acquaintances. Others were "high accountability" groups which met formally each week, and even more often on an informal basis. Consequently, our participation level went up. What is more, these small groups attracted different kinds of people than before.

If we had not reviewed our policy and allowed the rules to be challenged, we'd still be doing an okay job. But by reexamining our small-group rules and models, a greater percentage of our church family became connected, nurtured, taught, equipped, and employed in the workforce of the church.

That's the church-wide benefit. My leadership style was also affected for the better. My best laid plans for my group are now resubmitted and continually subject to God's interference and redirection by others. Christ is the Chief Shepherd of my group, and I am but an under-shepherd of his people.

Check-Up Quiz

Do you govern by policies or principles?

Take a few minutes today and examine the basis upon which you make decisions. A check-up quiz will help you to see what is ruling your group.

1. Do you like it when your group runs by standard operating procedures, or could you care less whether anyone accepts and adjusts to these norms?

2. Are you, or anyone else in your group, willing to "make mistakes" or "venture outside the lines"?

3. Is there any policy that no longer guides the group toward fulfilling its goals and mission, but has become more of a

stumbling block? (Are you prepared to change that policy today?)

4. What three non-negotiable principles come to mind as you consider how you govern your group?

5. Is there anything about the type of group your church sponsors, or about the one you're in now, that inadvertently limits the participation of unchurched or uninvolved people?

Chapter 6

"Thom's Top Ten": The Most Frequently Asked Questions

"Lots of people confuse bad management with destiny."
—**Ken Hubbard**

"To laugh often and much; to win the respect of intelligent people and the affection of children; to earn the appreciation of honest critics and endure then betrayal of false friends; to appreciate beauty; to find the best in others; to leave the world a little better, whether by a healthy child or a garden patch or a redeemed social condition; to know even one life has breathed easier because you have lived. This is to have succeeded."
—**Ralph Waldo Emerson**

With apologies to David Letterman, we consider here "Thom's Top Ten" most frequently asked questions. These FAQs (in no particular order) focus on typical problems that plague small groups. You're bound to find your most pressing question somewhere in this chapter. For example:

▶ "What do I do when no one (or very few) show up?"
▶ "How do I nurture my leaders so they don't drop out along the way?"
▶ "What do I do about the person who dominates my small group—and the person who won't open up?"
▶ "How can I recover (or keep) the interest of my small group?"

If this were an interactive medium and you were a colleague or apprentice of mine, we'd brainstorm together to solve these ten common problems. In our Pilgrimage Training Group seminars, we have the time and the vehicle to do that. But now I can only raise a few diagnostic questions, isolate a few tools you can use, and identify the variables that need to be lined up. I urge you to try them on for size now, or file them away for future reference in your small-group "preventive maintenance" schedule.

Problem 10

"I just started a new small group, but no one (or very few people) showed up."

An apprentice of mine was determined to start a new group in a neighborhood where none had been established before. She had sufficient skills to lead, possessed an understanding of the demands, and "owned" the mission of the church and its small-group ministry. But when she kicked off the new group, it failed to grow beyond the three people she began with. Dejected, she proclaimed her failure and excused herself from leadership.

Sound familiar? I have had a half dozen of those experiences myself and could relate to her feelings of defeat. From my numerous false starts in the past 20 years, I know some of the variables that must work together if a group is to enjoy life. Ask yourself—and those who didn't come or didn't come back— some of these critical questions:

✓ **Day and time.** Was your group scheduled on the right day to accommodate prospective members? Was the meeting time right? Too early, too late, too long? Often enough? Too often?

This timing factor came into play, dramatically, for one divorce recovery group I know. It started out slow—with four recruits, but fell off from there, by half and half again, until none of the original four returned. The two leaders had set up a top-notch video-based curriculum as an every other week support group, but the members couldn't keep track of which weeks were on and which were off.

When queried, the on-again, off-again members said they needed more regular and reliable input than the infrequent structure was providing. (One missed session, and it was a month between meetings.) The four different prospects who came to the third meeting of this reconstituted group decided then and there to meet every week, with no skipping. Another key to launching more successful groups, was their decision to move their meeting day from midweek to Sunday nights.

I'm told the group has flourished ever since and has graduated many alumni who started other divorce recovery groups.

✓ **Meeting place.** Is it easily accessible? With ample, convenient parking? How many steps to climb? Can it be accessed by a person confined to a wheelchair or using crutches? Is the home or meeting place in an area the prospective group members would deem safe? Would a person feel safe walking to and from his or her car in the dark? If the meeting place is in an apartment or other multi-unit housing, is the noise level distracting? Are pets distracting? (Can they be put away during the meeting?)

The aforementioned divorce care group also had to choose a place which was conducive to their ministry objectives. The choice came down to meeting in a Sunday school room in their church for an hour before worship, or in a cozy family room at the leaders' home. The latter had the fireplace ambiance and kitchen amenities that made others feel right at home, something that displaced single homemakers needed.

☑ **Prospecting.** Ever wonder where to recruit people for your small group? A growing small group ministry will want to expand its pool of prospects. My friend Kent Odor points to five "circles of influence" everyone has, from which we can recruit or invite people. He calls them the five Fs. If you look at your life through these five circles of influence, the crowd from which to recruit grows significantly.

▶ Fellowship: Those who we are in relationship with or see at church;
▶ Friends: That is, neighbors and classmates;
▶ Family: Spouse, parents, children, relatives;
▶ Fun: Those with whom we play sports or attend games or share hobbies;
▶ Factory: While you may not work in a factory, there are people at work who are seeking, or have had previous church background and are not currently in fellowship.

Problem 9

"How do I nurture my leaders (host/hostess, apprentices) so they don't drop out along the way?"

The idea of nurturing people who volunteer their home, or who are in training with you, may be a foreign idea. After all, aren't there enough people who really need your attention and care? The healthy ones can take care of themselves, right?

Yes and no. Just as couples bring different lists of what

they need into a marriage (some spouses are "lower maintenance" and some are "higher maintenance"), the same is tru
of your team of group leaders and your leaders within each
group. Some will need hand-holding at crisis points, while
low-maintenance types can go a long time between "check
up" visits.

☑ **Maintenance schedules.** Plan and maintain a minimum
maintenance schedule so that all small-group leaders will fe‹
valued in their position as host/hostess or as apprentices. Bu
once you learn who needs more maintenance (nurture) to
keep going, make an attempt to see that those needs are
met—but not necessarily always by you.

I have found that most people need just a little attention
and encouragement to keep on track and to be content in
relationships. In keeping with the principle of preventative
maintenance, the human soul needs regular (though often
brief) contact and reassurance that things are going in the
right direction. Even low-maintenance people, who need littl‹
input from you to keep going, still need encouragement.

Encouragement is like sweet nectar to a thirsty person an‹
like oxygen to a fire. Many people in your groups are greatly
malnourished, even starving or suffocating, in that regard.
Without some encouragement along the way, they die.

Time spent in discouraging situations at work (downsizing
backbiting, or other related disasters) means that your leader‹
come to the team meeting at church drained of vital energy
and look to you (and God) to refill their cup. Forced to shake
off the events of the day and week, the average Jack and Jill
will find it tough to shift gears and focus on their relationship
with God or the answers to prayers they may have received
during the week. But it's your job to stir up this hope by "not
neglecting to meet together, as is the habit of some" (Hebrews
10:25). Remind Jack and Jill (and yourself) of the valuable par
that group leaders play in caring for others.

If you overlook this need, or rationalize it away because it
doesn't fit your leadership style or personality type, then you'r‹
setting yourself up for ongoing problems. You'll have to recrui‹
more leaders to replace the ones who may have been well-
trained and very productive. If you are willing to learn shep-
herding from Jesus, the Chief Shepherd, encouraging Jack an‹
Jill will become a lifestyle and a relationship, not a program.

The gift and ministry of encouragement: of course, the

"Jesus style" of gentle servant-leadership runs contrary to current cultural standards for leadership. Scripture calls for shepherds, while today's culture calls for hard-nosed drivers whose bottom line is "getting it done"—no matter what it takes. The apostle Paul saw encouragement as a spiritual gift and as a special mission that God's leaders are sent on. Barnabas, Timothy, Epaphroditus, and Paul each had ministries of encouragement.

My experience with people in small groups bears out the truth of an experiment I heard about. It tested this theory that encouragement brings out the best in people.

> Ten adults were each given a puzzle to solve. The puzzle was the same for each person. After they worked on them, they turned them in and were given the results, but the results were fictitious. Half of them were told they had done well, getting 7 of 10 right. The other half were told they had done poorly, with 7 of 10 wrong. Then they were all given another puzzle, each receiving the same puzzle. The half who had been told they did well the first time, did better. The half who were told they did badly the first time, did worse. Criticism, though given falsely, ruined them.

I've heard it said, "People tend to become what the most important person in their lives think they will become." That follows what the inventor Henry Ford once said, "Whether you think you can or can't, you're right." I have yet to meet a person who did not put forth more effort in pursuit of excellence under a spirit of encouragement and approval than a spirit of criticism or dissatisfaction.

Problem 8

"What do I do about the person who dominates my small group—and the person I can't get to open up?"

When a person acts up or displays controlling behavior, deal with it immediately by redirecting the group back to the matter at hand. Pray for the wisdom to discern when personal needs and issues need to be the focus, and when you should stay the course on the group agenda. Later, after the formal time of the group meeting is over, you will have an opportunity to approach the person while the issue is still fresh, and share one-to-one (without embarrassing anyone) your perception of the disruptive or controlling behavior.

Reconfirm that person's valuable contributions to the group, and validate everyone's opportunity and right to share their views without being argued with or badgered about it. Your goal is to protect the individual's integrity, while not giving up the leadership, purpose, or principles of the group.

I once led a group consisting of people who did not seem to fit into any other groups—a group of "misfits," you might say. They were young college age men and women who loved "alternative" music, dress, and hairstyles. This odd group was serious about their faith, with no religious pretense or cover-up. We had wonderful and lively discussions, but my job as leader quickly changed from teacher-leader, to facilitator-traffic cop, paving the way for as many group members to share their input as possible. The "Type A" personalities in our group dominated the discussion, if I allowed, while the two less assertive persons in our group needed to be drawn out. Let me introduce you to some cases in point.

Skeptical Skip
Skip has one view on life in the group: "It won't work," or "It will never last." He has decided that life is, at best, something to "get through." Something in Skip's life has deeply disappointed him and has made him afraid to hope. Skip can undermine your best plans, so it's easy to lose patience with him, but what he most needs is encouragement. Remind him that though life is tough, God has a wonderful plan for each of us and will cover us with grace, blessing, and strength to endure and to overcome.

Advice-for-free Ann
Ann is the resident counselor with great insights for all that ails you. Her language is often liberally sprinkled with shoulds, oughts, and have-to's. Remind Ann that the group is not looking for counsel, but rather for love, acceptance, and forgiveness demonstrated by availability, encouragement, and prayer.

Professor Pam
Pam shows up with concordance, Bible encyclopedia, and commentaries in hand. She always wants to go deeper, but forgets that application and transformation are your goals. Assure her that Bible study is part of your group's agenda,

but that it is a means to an end: transformation. Explain that you want to help those who are reading a Bible passage for the first time to understand it correctly, without overwhelming them with more information than they can digest. If Pam is receptive, you might channel her gift for study in a constructive direction. Enlist her support to research a passage and provide written notes for group members to take home with them if they wish.

Dogmatic Don

Don combines intolerance with imperiousness, pronouncing the last word on every subject. The religious blanket that Don throws over the group can be tough to discard. Take some time to pray for him until you can approach him with sensitivity and compassion. Gently explain that he is coming across with an all-knowing attitude that discourages others in the group to think for themselves. If you restate your group's ground rules at the beginning of each meeting, Don may remember to respect other members' views better.

Silent Sue

Sue seemed interested enough, but never entered into the discussion. After weeks of inviting her to participate (asking, "Sue, what is your view on this issue?"), but getting no response, I went to her after the meeting one evening. Following small talk, I asked, "You've been here every week since we started and you look interested, but we haven't heard your input. Are you comfortable with this group?"

She remarked that she was, but just needed more time to feel like she could join in. I told her to take whatever time she needed, but also suggested that I would, from time to time, invite her comments. I also began sitting directly across from her in the group, so she would get the most eye contact from me and hopefully would see that as a green light to jump in.

She remained silent for another few months, but I persisted in inviting her to participate and spoke with her a few times before or after group to reinforce our desire for her to join in. In time she did. Her thoughts were articulate and timely. With perseverance on both parts, Sue became a fully-functioning member of the group.

Jabbering Joe

Joe required extra energy, as well, but a very different approach. This young man had little control over his mouth.

Whenever a thought crossed his mind, it ran through his mouth, with no regard for the subject at hand! Significant self-esteem issues were evident. His misbehavior demanded a more proactive, assertive response than was necessary with Sue.

I started the second meeting with a five-minute teaching on "group-life," spelling out how we needed to honor the various gifts and expressions of the body of Christ within our group, and that we showed honor by listening to one another. That speech had its intended effect for one week.

Then Joe was up to his old stuff again. I decided to invite him to sit next to me each week, where I could limit eye-contact (that he might find encouraging) and nudge his arm (to interrupt his train of thought). Once I got him to pause, I'd jump in to redirect the discussion ("Mary, what is your view on this issue?"). Only then could some people get a chance to speak.

After a few more weeks of this, I finally confronted Joe in private about his behavior. I reminded him that I liked him and valued him as a member of the group. I then shared my perception that his continuous talking made other group members uncomfortable, and caused one person to quit the group. I then asked Joe to take a "leave of absence" from our group and meet for peer counseling at our church over the next several weeks. After extensive interviews and prayer, this peer minister would then return him to our group or ask him to seek additional counseling at a local Christian counseling center.

At first Joe was hurt and angry. (Who wouldn't be?) But because he recognized I was committed to him and this was not an attempt to abandon him, he agreed to go. This was a hard situation, but in order for Joe to be healed, renewed, retooled, and eventually reconciled to the group—and in order to protect the group—I had to take the risk. Joe got help for a problem he had struggled with for years, and the group saw mercy in action toward someone who behaved outside the norm.

Many people hide their insecurities, their deepest fears or hurts, behind their behaviors. Be gentle when you approach them and be willing to follow through. Each personality in your group has potential if brought under the lordship of Christ. Your job, as leader of the group, is to encourage each individual to grow up in Christ (Ephesians 4:15).

Also, bear in mind that people with deep-seated emotional

or psychological problems will need referral elsewhere. If you, as the small-group leader, suspect that the problem is too big to handle yourself or with peer counseling, call for advice from the minister of small groups, who can then help you determine whether the person should remain in your group or be referred out for counseling or therapy.

Problem 7

"What can I do to recover (or keep) the interest of my small group?"

For many reasons, some of them good, your members may lose interest in the group. They might even become, as one care group leader told me, the "I-don't-care" group.

☑ **The leader's lack of preparation.** The main reason people quit coming, I believe, is due to our own lack of preparation. Our members can't help but compare the small-group leader's presentation with the excellent presentations they see at work, at school, or even on TV. Such comparisons make us look bad. Lack of preparation on our part says, "You don't deserve my best, just whatever I can scrape together."

Whether you are unable or unwilling to prepare, may I encourage you to make group presentation a higher priority. Perhaps you suffer from a lack of planning or discipline in time management. Many tools (books, training tapes, seminars) can help to train a leader who will stir up the interest of any small group. Remember, whatever we are called to do, we do as unto the Lord.

☑ **The leader's lack of presentation skills.** You may understand how to prepare, but group interest suffers from your inability to present a lesson or to lead the agenda in a way that holds their attention. It might be helpful to ask someone who has those skills to observe you leading a group meeting. Ask for constructive criticism and encouragement afterward. You may also want to speak with your pastor about a skill-training session for small-group leaders on the issues of preparation and presentation.

☑ **Poor choice of curriculum.** Is your curriculum meeting the felt needs of your group? I ask the question this way, because we often need to meet the felt needs of people (as they perceive them) before we have the right to help them with their real need (which may not be apparent to them).

Jesus often dealt with felt needs such as feeding the hungry, healing the sick, and casting out demons before ministering to their hearts. He knew the secret of getting someone's attention before he told them the truth.

It may be wise to speak with your pastor, small-group coordinator, or to visit your local Christian bookstore for good curriculum and small-group resources. Good materials will have four well-designed modules:

▶ *The Beginning.* This module is designed to open up the session by sharing our history and stories.
▶ *The Text.* This module focuses our attention on God's Word.
▶ *Understanding the Text.* This module helps us to observe what the text says, and interpret what it means.
▶ *Applying the Text.* This module connects our lives to God's Word.

When examining the suitability of a particular curriculum, you can ask yourself these four questions:

▶ Do the questions help me understand what the Bible passage said *to its original hearers and readers?*
▶ Do the questions help me understand what the Bible passage is saying *to me today?*
▶ Will the questions work *in my small group?* (Could I answer these questions? Or does it take special expertise?)
▶ Used over several weeks, will this study guide help us develop *into the group we want to become?*

Problem 6

"I don't know what's expected of me as a leader."

We are all asked to serve in positions from time to time that lack any clear set of written expectations. The inevitable result? Frustration, because we don't accomplish what the supervisor wants to get done.

Having learned the hard way, I do not ask anyone to serve under my direction without a clearly written job description. Job descriptions are essential in communicating expectations to a potential leader. This tool can also be used to help an errant leader return to the intended behavior and principles that are outlined in the job description. The following criteria are included in most good job descriptions:

- ► *Position/title* (Is it a functional title, or a high-falutin' one?)
- ► *List of responsibilities* (Are they reasonable? Measurable?)
- ► *Term of service* (Does it expire or is it renewable?)
- ► *Lines of communication* (Who reports to, or checks off with, whom?)
- ► *Resources* (Anything to help you get the job done?)
- ► *Delegated authority* (Avoid "all responsibility and no authority.")
- ► *Benefits* (Anything stipulated specifically for leaders?)

Look for these prerequisites, which are descriptive of small-group leaders:

- ► *Character*—a love for Jesus and a consistent godly walk
- ► *Commitment*—to the local church and its leaders
- ► *Giftedness*—a call from God and a commitment to serve

For more specific job descriptions of the small-group leader, the apprentice or assistant leader, and the host or hostess, I refer you to appendix B.

Problem 5

"Our group is unclear about its direction and commitment."

This problem is similar to when the leader does not know what the job expectations are. When small-group members are not sure about their responsibilities and commitments, the problem is resolved by seeking clarity in writing, preferably in the form of a covenant. Every small group should have a covenant, or contract, among members. This should be reviewed and renegotiated periodically, especially when lack of direction or commitment becomes a problem. Ground rules will vary, but some essential elements are found in most small groups. A sample covenant, including these key elements, is reproduced in appendix C.

Problem 4

"The leader's responsibility feels too burdensome and is weighing me down."

I often hear questions from leaders referring to the pressure they feel from expectations and needs of folks in their group. This pressure often reflects a problem with boundaries or limits, as well as with the need to control. These problems stem from attitudes and assumptions that are addressed in chapters 2 and 3.

If you need more help in this regard, and cannot distinguish your God-given responsibilities from the extra burdens you have taken on, go to the New Testament. Ask yourself, "Which of these responsibilities am I rightly taking, and trusting God to share the burden?" "Which of these burdens have I taken on myself, but which are rightly none of my business?"

We are responsible to _____ one another:
▶ love (John 13:34)
▶ be devoted to and honor (Romans 12 :10)
▶ live in harmony with (Romans 12:16)
▶ serve (Galatians 5:13)
▶ meet with (Hebrews 10:24)
▶ submit to (Ephesians 5:21)
▶ bear with and forgive (Colossians 3:13)

However, we are *not* responsible for other people's _____:
▶ happiness
▶ problems
▶ decisions
▶ behavior

Failing to abide by healthy biblical principles and boundaries such as these, we can slip easily into controlling, codependent behavior and resentment. If you find yourself in a situation where you have been the caretaker, reevaluate your relationship. Are you hooked by your own need to be needed? Do you sometimes think that only you can help this person?

If so, you are in a way playing God in this person's life and robbing him of the opportunity to make godly, healthy choices for himself. If he needs education, information, or counseling, talk to your pastor about where he can get help. Put some distance between you and him. You can respond in an adult manner, with compassion, without owning his problems.

When someone asks me what I think she should do about a certain problem or situation, I usually ask her, "What do you think you should do?" or "What do you suppose the Scriptures say about this?" In so doing, I shift responsibility back to her, where it belongs, while remaining empathetic and supportive.

Do not be controlled by someone else's guilt or shaming tactics. If that happens, explain to the person how her behavior is controlling and talk to a pastoral leader for additional insight and direction.

Even after following the above guidelines, a leader will sometimes get into a situation that would overwhelm even a trained professional. I often found myself in such situations when I first led groups. Sometimes it was a behavior issue. Other times it was a theological question which exposed an area of ignorance. Often it was group dynamics. Through it all, I learned two valuable lessons that helped me when I felt like I was in over my head:

Simply say, "I don't know." When asked a question that stumps you, regardless of how humiliating that may be, have enough integrity, courage, and humility to say "I don't know." Then shut up, go home to the library, to your pastor—wherever you can find a sufficient or correct answer—and bring that back to the group as soon as you can.

Get help for yourself. Twenty years ago, there was not much material published for small groups, even less for trouble-shooting. I bought whatever I could, but I was also determined to ask people questions until help arrived. Sometimes I became a pest, but I felt my group was important enough to risk this. Now in my church we have set up a training system for each small-group leader. This system includes low-level peer support, pastors-on-call, and top-of-the-line Christian professionals in various fields outside the church. If your church lacks such a system, you should lobby for one.

Problem 3

"What roles should I play in facilitating necessary change or future growth?"

I have been asked many times by group leaders, "I am feeling pressure to change my leadership style or to obtain different skills. There seems to be a need for change in me or in my group. How should I respond?"

Generally speaking, a group moves from infancy to adolescence to adulthood to closure. Another way to look at the life cycle of groups is the Pilgrimage process of formation (6-12 weeks), nurture (6-10 weeks), equipping (10-20 weeks), and deployment (6-8 weeks). The length of each of these "cycles" or seasons will vary from group to group, but it can be predicted, contracted for, and facilitated. These changes bring pressure on the leader to adapt a leadership style that helps the group as it goes through that phase of growth. In broad terms, the two leadership styles needed are "authoritative" and "facilitative."

Leadership needs to flow from authoritative to facilitative as a group begins to form its identity. The leader should exhibit more authority at the early phase of a group's development. Then, in the group's later stages of development, the leader should move to a more facilitative role through delegating, coaching, empowering, and building consensus. The comparison below highlights the differences between these two roles:

Authoritative Leader's Role
- ▶ tell
- ▶ direct
- ▶ decide
- ▶ solve problems
- ▶ set goals
- ▶ use authority to get things done

Facilitative Leader's Role
- ▶ listen and ask questions
- ▶ direct group process
- ▶ share decision making
- ▶ teach
- ▶ delegate
- ▶ empower others

The diagram below shows how this relationship evolves over time.[1]

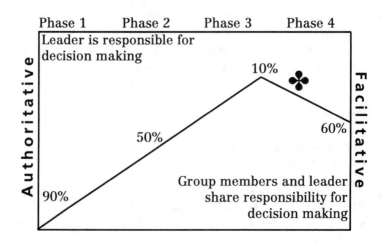

Problem 2

"What can (or should) be done about children of small-group members?"

Child care is an important issue to deal with head on. It can lead to considerable frustration for parents of small children—and for the non-parents in your group. It can be the difference between people coming or staying away. Here are the solutions that we have used with some success:

► Trade off child care with parents of a small group that meets at another time.
► If your host's home is large enough and has a separate safe area—a basement rec room or family room—then rotate your own people out of the group discussion to watch them.
► If your whole group is in favor, let the children participate in the group. Be aware that having children in the group radically changes some of the group process and the benefits to the adults.
► Hire one or more older kids to care for the children. They can either act as babysitters, or they can work with prepared materials that design activities with an educational purpose.
► If all the groups are in close proximity to the church, you can offer organized childcare and ministry for all groups that meet on a particular evening. (We have found that making child care the responsibility of the group is often the better option.)
► If a minority of the members have children, take up a monthly offering in the group, so they can afford to hire child care at home without assuming a large financial burden.

This challenge can be best dealt with if it is approached with all the creativity of your small group!

Problem 1

"Should we 'close' our group or remain 'open' to newcomers?"

"Open" simply means that a newcomer can visit or join the group at any time. "Closed" means that you have sufficient reason to restrict access to newcomers—usually for the sake of accountability, confidentiality, and building community.

This issue should be included in your small group covenant. If not, have the group work it out with input from a pastor. At the pastoral staff level, I have found it wise to place some parameters on open/closed groups. I generally ask that all groups be open for at least the first three or four times they meet. Then they can close for a period of six months. At that point, the leader meets with the pastor of small groups to talk about group health, goals, outreach, etc. The pastor "takes the temperature" of the group.

In determining its degree of health, the pastor and small-group leader make one of two recommendations: (a) either allow it to remain a closed group; or (b) ask the group to reopen for a period of time, allowing new people to check out the group. In either event, allow current group members to then leave the group, if they so desire, as part of your decision to review or rewrite your group's covenant.

You may have questions that are not specifically stated here in our "Top Ten." But the system of checks and balances suggested here, together with the ability to ask good diagnostic questions, has proven to be beneficial to hundreds of groups I have counseled over the years.

---

[1]Adapted from *How to Lead Work Teams: Facilitation Skills,* by Fran Ross (San Diego: Pfeiffer & Co., 1991).

Chapter 7

When Failure Is
Your Next Step to Success

"Victory goes to the player who makes the next-to-last mistake."
—Savielly Grigorievitch Tartakower, chessmaster

*"A doctor can bury his mistakes
but an architect can only advise his clients to plant vines."*
—Frank Lloyd Wright, architect

"If Stupidity got us into this mess, then why can't it get us out?"
—Will Rogers, comedian

*"Far better it is to dare mighty things, to win mighty triumphs
even though checkered by failure, than to rank with those poor
spirits who neither enjoy nor suffer much, because they live in
the gray twilight that knows neither victory nor defeat."*
—Theodore Roosevelt, president

"We made too many wrong mistakes."
—Yogi Berra, NY Yankees catcher

"Failure is the opportunity to begin again more intelligently."
—John Maxwell, preacher

I love celebrating failure! Long ago, after missing the mark
while attempting a major objective of ministry, I fell into sudden
despair and a flood of self-pity. ("I never will get this. I just don't
have what it takes.") An older, wiser friend said, "Who said you
failed? And why did you give them the right to determine what
you've gained from your circumstances?"

An elephant never forgets

I began to protest, saying he did not understand. But he persisted. By the time our discussion was over, he had called me
an "elephant" and made his point with this often-told parable:

When they are young, baby elephants are heavily
chained to stakes driven deep in the ground. Pull as they

might, they remain fully tethered. Soon, the baby elephant becomes discouraged and stops pulling. It learns to stay put. Even as adults the lesson holds great power over the full-grown elephant. The stake which is still the same size it was when the elephant was small, and could now be easily torn loose by this powerful behemoth, holds the multi-ton animal because of the strength of the lesson it learned.

In a sense, discouragement makes us all like those elephants. Although we have the power we didn't have as children to pursue our dreams, discouragement keeps us from using that creative power. We feel chained down by our unrealized expectations.

Failure can teach us much, especially if we persevere through discouragement, evaluate the lesson to be learned, and respond accordingly. Making mistakes is not wrong. The only wrong mistakes are the ones we fail to learn from.

The baseball pitcher who serves up a home run ball because he pitched to the power hitter's strength has made a big mistake, but not a wrong mistake. An egregiously wrong mistake would be for the pitcher to keep throwing to the same spot, making no adjustments, and suffering the same result. Any pitcher who fails to learn from his mistakes doesn't last long.

Conversely, only those pitchers willing to take risks, try new pitches, and challenge hitters to hit their best stuff will last. It also helps if your manager (pastor) is willing to tolerate mistakes by pitchers who are still on a learning curve. If one mistake gets you an early exit, what do you learn from that, other than a fear of making mistakes?

The same is true in small-group ministry led by the managers of God's flock. Small-group coordinators and pastors should build a positive and healthy atmosphere that allows—even encourages—people to take risks and make mistakes. (Gulp!) The good news is that fear of failure can be unlearned by God's grace. Unlearn this fear, and that will develop your pitchers, increase the team ministry, and advance the kingdom of God.

If at first you don't succeed, try failing again

If we are not failing, then we are not trying anything new.

Failure is a good yardstick to measure our willingness to risk.

When confronted by his contemporaries and encouraged to quit his pursuit of a suitable element for his electric light bulb, Thomas Edison did not give up. (Thank God for that, or we might still be fumbling around in the dark by the light of gas lamps.) On the occasion of his 5,000th attempt to invent the incandescent light bulb, Edison is known to have said words to this effect, "I am not a failure. Rather, I have successfully identified and eliminated 5,000 ways that do not work, which brings me 5,000 steps closer to discovering the one way that will work."

That being the case, you and I need to fail more often!

In starting the training organization I now direct, the Pilgrimage Training Group, we had to overcome many barriers that appeared insurmountable. I was living in a city where we knew few people, operating without sufficient financial backing, attempting a faith venture that wasn't built around a single big-name personality. Many close friends and associates told me I would not succeed, that people would not pay to attend a seminar led by anyone other than a well-known Christian leader.

What got me through was a confidence that God was calling me to do this, a willingness to abandon my "reputation" to his hands, and my wife, Chris, who supported me through every step of the process. We are now presenting over 100 seminars a year in North America in wonderful host churches, training thousands of pastors and leaders. Our seminar leaders are pastoral leaders from 22 different denominations, who have extensive backgrounds in small-group ministry, but no huge reputations! God is willing to bless faith.

I can't count the number of times I have trained and released a small-group leader—full of energy, zeal, and courage, ready to start a new group—who then hits the wall of rejection. After a few weeks of trying to fly, he returns to me disheartened, lacking hope of ever trying again. I often lead such dejected leaders through a mental checklist of diagnostic questions:

▶ Was the problem "right meeting time and day, but wrong place"? or,

▶ Was it "right day and neighborhood, but wrong curriculum"? or,

▶ Was it "right subject matter, good host home and timing, but wrong day"?

Then I go on to say, "These and many more factors are all possibilities, so why don't we examine the mix a little more, then restart again in a few weeks, okay?"

Invariably I give the discouraged leader some encouraging words from Scripture. I rely heavily on David's words of encouragement to Solomon, for example, which are appropriate for anyone called of God and facing an unfinished task:

> *"Be strong and courageous, and do the work. Do not be afraid or discouraged, for the LORD God, my God, is with you. He will not fail you or forsake you until all the work for the service of the temple of the LORD is finished"*
> *(1 Chronicles 28:20).*

More often than not, the new chemistry works better, the group takes off, and my leader is encouraged and re-energized by God's assurances of his protection and provision.

Cleaning up messy mistakes

Don't let the spirit of procrastination or discouragement deter you from finishing the work God gave you to do. Procrastination is actually the fear of succeeding, which is what will happen if you move ahead now.

Normally, I hate messes. And I do my best to clean them up. But I procrastinate about messes that seem culturally and perfectly acceptable to me. Take the mess piled on my desk, for example. Take it. I am very uncomfortable about cleaning it all up. I call these vertical lopsided piles "creative sorting"—a new approach I'm developing which will one day replace filing. As anyone who shares my unease will tell you, "A clean desk is the sign of sick mind." By that standard, I'm pretty healthy.

Then there are messes that must be cleaned up. A baby's messy diapers must be removed. The debris-filled yard needs a spring cleaning. The house needs a clean-up before company comes over. These messes are a natural part of life. They happen naturally, if irregularly, so you may as well plan on them, and don't lose any sleep fretting over them.

Other messes are caused by human mistakes or accidents (not our own) or by unforeseen circumstances ("Stuff happens!"). Although we cannot prepare for these misfortunes, it is our very inability to control these messes (or even learn from them) that frustrates us so.

A third group of messy mistakes are those that result from our own lack of planning, laziness, or failure to follow through. When that happens, take a step back, and analyze the situation long enough to determine what went wrong, respond to the current situation with grace and dignity, then do what you can to avoid making the same mess again.

Some messes are traumatic, as when someone's life hangs in the balance. But even in these circumstances, I have heard a doctor say, "It depends on God and the person's will to live." A small-group ministry can be like that. When we invest in another person, and it "blows up in our face," the outcome often "depends on God and our will to live," so to speak. Our willingness to take the medicine, take the time to recover and rehabilitate, and take stock of what went wrong and what resources will make us well—that makes all the difference in the "life and death" of any ministry.

A few probing questions and comments will help you evaluate what happened and why, how to clean up the mess, and then to recover wholeness.

'etting with God's game plan

A crucial part of leading any small group successfully is to know and understand the plan. What is that plan? If you do not have one, take time now to pray and ask our Father for his plan. Speak with your pastor or other leaders to help you develop the plan. This plan for success should include many failed attempts, à la Thomas Edison. The plan also consists, in large part, of God's grace, as well as church values, mission priorities, and personal convictions.

Do you understand the balance of those components? I realize that God always plays a bigger part than we do. But I am also reminded of a saying passed down to me from my Irish grandfather, which puts me in my proper role: "If you pray for potatoes, pick up a hoe."

It's one thing to know God's plan of salvation and his plan for the Church. But it's another thing to do that plan. A saying common to Alcoholics Anonymous, and other recovery groups, also speaks of any small-group ministry plan: "It works if you work it!" Simple but profound.

The plan is not the goal, but rather a set of parameters and assumptions you can use to help you achieve your goals. Are you staying within those parameters? Do you have enough definition to have well-established boundaries?

Falling off, getting hurt, and getting back on

If this is true, and you've fallen spla-a-a-t in the middle of a small-group venture, then admit it—to God, to yourself, to one other person, and to your group (if it's still together). Determine what you can do to make amends and pick up the pieces. People matter most to God, so whatever you can do to recognize the hurt that others may have suffered, do that. You may need help in recovery yourself. That may mean binding up some wounds and starting over, just as you did when you were learning to ride a bike after you took your first nasty fall.

Remember how you first learned to ride a two-wheeler? I remember all the joy and exhilaration, fear and pain, of that long-awaited day when my father finally took off the training wheels from my bike. Suddenly, the bike seemed a little bigger, a little faster, a little more ominous. My dad held onto the back of the seat, to secure and to steady me. Knowing he was back there gave me security.

At some point my father let go and did not tell me. I don't know if I went 20 feet or 200 feet on my first solo run. But when I turned around, he was not there. Exhilaration set in again. I'm riding my bike! Then reality took hold, and panic set in. I'm going to die! I'll crash. That'll be the end of me and my bike.

I wobbled and over-corrected. Then a valuable lesson hit me: *It's not the fall that hurts you; it's the sudden stop on the pavement.*

I laid in a crumpled mass until Dad got there to untwist the body-wrapped-in-bike pretzel. He held me. Mom came running up, offered me motherly words, strokes, and kisses, and took me in the house for repairs.

A short while later, after he had straightened out the handlebars and fenders, Dad invited me to try it again. I thought to myself, *Get on that thing again? After what it just did to me? You gotta be crazy.*

Dad waited patiently for me. Eventually I came outdoors— but just to check on the bike. He coaxed me back on the bike to try again. Soon he "launched me." There I was, riding a two-wheeler, like all the big boys on the block! My dad had convinced me that I needed to get back on the bike and to try again, despite the pain of skinned knees and a bruised ego.

earning from our mistakes and moving on

How will you deal with your bicycle wreck? Is your response typically *reactive* (inclined toward pouting, despair, rejection, even revenge)? Or are you typically *proactive* in response to crises or adversity?

A crisis brings out a proactive response in those who determine in advance what they will do. Determine now that you will actively and prayerfully review all contributing factors to see what God is teaching you. Determine now that you will do whatever it takes to remedy the situation—whether that means repentance, restitution, reconciliation, or whatever. Do these things, and you will profit from all that God has to teach you from this adversity.

I remember more than once finding myself neck-deep in a problem and determining that I could not, or would not, attempt this again. I did not understand who I was and what emotional baggage I was carrying around. Nor did I understand who my heavenly Father was, and what he had already done about that past experience and hurt. Somehow, in my subconscious, I had decided that this current crisis would expose me to more pain, which I wanted to avoid at all costs. I had fallen off my bicycle, and I did not want to get on that thing again.

Some of the best learning experiences in small-group ministry have been my worst mistakes and failures. I've learned to celebrate failure in order to see that the process is as important as my goal. Setting goals and successfully attaining them—that end result is important. But living the process is equally important.

That process involves change, pain, joy, and growth. If God is indeed for us and his plans are good—"plans to prosper you and not to harm you, plans to give you hope and a future" (Jeremiah 29:11)—then I can confidently trust my situation to a good God. I can then choose to make the best of whatever comes my way. Whenever I choose the easy way out, I may experience short-term gain, but I miss out on God's long-term benefits. Conversely, whenever I choose the road less traveled, that way appears narrow and risky at first, but the long-term benefits make it worth every sacrifice.

I now find myself turning more and more over to God and receiving from him the guidance, grace, and wisdom that he promises in his Word (Proverbs 2:10–11): "Then you will understand what is right and just and fair—every good path. For wisdom will enter your heart, and knowledge will be pleasant to your soul. Discretion will protect you, and under-standing will guard you."

Okay, so you've made a few mistakes, experienced a few minor mishaps. Even a few big ones. We all do. Now what?

As I see it, you can quietly retire, stoically resign, or try shifting blame—all reactive mode responses. Or you can be proactive, take a step back, examine your situation to learn from it, and then go deeper.

Going deeper—in reality, recovery, renewal, and risk

I used to think that living the Christian life grounded in God's Word meant that I wouldn't ever be deceived, that I would always love my wife and children and my "neighbors as myself," and that turning things over to God would be instinc-tive and instantly rewarded. I thought being a Christian was the nice, safe road to go. But then I had a dream a few years ago, which I believe was from God, and it challenged me to change my walk before God and others. I remember very few of my dreams, but this one remains vivid. It was about me and my walk with God.

> Walking through a wooded area, I came upon a lagoon of peaceful water. Thirsty, I bent down to drink from a small teaspoon in hand. Then I heard a voice from heaven say-ing, "Why do you drink from this dead pool with a little spoon? Aren't you thirsty for more, for me? Look up and see the flow of life that is a fast moving river."
>
> I looked up and there it was, a small distance away. Walking over to the river, I knelt down and again took out my teaspoon to get a drink. This time the water was cool and refreshing. It made me feel alive. Then I heard the voice again, "I want you to drink deeply of Me. I want you to wade out into the water where you can drink and be washed in the life that comes from Me."
>
> So I waded out into the cool refreshing river until the water lapped around my ankles. I could sense joy and healing in the waters, and I wanted to stay put and bathe in the "safety" of the shallows. But I heard the same voice beckoning me, "Come out into the deep, where you will be in over your head, where your feet

cannot touch the bottom, where the current will wash over you and carry you along in its power."

I balked, "Lord, I am afraid to go into the deep, I am afraid of being out of control and losing my footing." And he beckoned me still, "Come out into the deep, where the flow of My Spirit will carry you, and you can learn to rest in Me and know My ways. My power and plan will sustain you!"

At that point, I awoke to reality. But my reality had changed, or at least my approach to God's reality has.

From time to time, I still struggle to let go and to wade out into the deep. But often, especially in the midst of small-group community, I feel so supported, encouraged, and unconditionally loved that I will venture a little farther out into the water. Sometimes I "courageously" venture deeper still, until the water covers my knees, but not too far that I can't run back to the shallows, where I feel safe.

To this day, I can still hear my Master calling. God is not in a hurry and is not upset at my lack of faith. That encourages me.

I believe God is calling his people to take the risky steps into the deep. Why not take the ultimate step yourself? Go! And maybe, just maybe, you'll find your small group already knee-deep in this fresh encounter with God, wading in with you.

Then the angel showed me the river of the water of life, as clear as crystal, flowing from the throne of God and of the Lamb down the middle of the great street of the city. On each side of the river stood the tree of life, bearing twelve crops of fruit, yielding its fruit every month. And the leaves of the tree are for the healing of the nations. (Revelation 22:1–2)

Developing a Personal Mission Statement

Vision and mission are interrelated but different.

Mission is a general statement of ministry or personal objectives; it is a philosophical statement that sets a "track to run on"; it is a guideline for life.

Vision is a specific, detailed statement of direction and uniqueness; it is strategic. It sets parameters and boundaries for what you do, in what or whom you invest your time, energy, and money.

A meaningful personal mission statement contains two elements:

☑ The first is what you want to be—what character strengths you want to have, what qualities you want to develop.

☑ The second is what you want to do—what you want to accomplish, what contributions you want to make.

An example of a personal mission statement is:

► My mission is to be a leader in my family, in my neighborhood, my community and country.

► I desire to be a faithful, supportive husband, a caring father who encourages my children to develop their unique personality and talents; to be a mentor to my peers and a role-model to my countrymen.

► I am committed to being loyal, faithful, and honest, to walking in integrity and character.

► I am committed to be a person of purpose, committed to my core values of being a person of grace and mercy; of being generous with my resources, being willing to invest in others and draw the best out of them.

► I am committed to being a wise manager of my life and ministry.

► I am committed to pursue truth and to exhibit the evidence of the kingdom of God in all my endeavors.

► I am committed to achieve my personal best, to encourage others to grow, to take risks and to reach beyond the status quo.

An example of a family mission statement is:

Our Family Mission

▶ To love each other
▶ To help each other
▶ To believe in each other
▶ To wisely use our time, talents, and resources to bless others
▶ To worship together throughout our lives

Developing Job Descriptions for Small-Group Leaders

Group leader

▶ Prays for the group members and potential apprentices

▶ Plans and conducts small-group meetings, implementing some aspect of the six elements of a healthy group:
  • Care and nurture
  • Teaching
  • Worship and/or prayer
  • Outreach and service
  • Develop a vision for the group and leader development
  • Telling the gospel message, sharing of testimonies

▶ Helps the group form and commit to a group covenant or ground rules

▶ Shepherds the members of the group

▶ Develops and empowers apprentices

▶ Meets with/encourages the leadership team, host[ess] and apprentice[s]

▶ Communicates with and submits reports to the coach or small-groups pastor

Apprentice group leader

▶ Helps and supports the group leader

▶ Carries out any of the tasks assigned by the leader

▶ Helps the leader to care for the group members

▶ Meets regularly with the leadership team for prayer, to discuss the group's progress and development, and to brainstorm

▶ Attends leader training and leadership community meetings

3. *Host/hostess*

▶ Provides a home that is nonrestrictive, and large enough to hold 12–15 people comfortably

▶ If needed, provides a safe space for children, far enough away from parents to allow privacy

▶ Helps and supports the group leader

▶ Provides a neat, clean, warm, and inviting atmosphere for the group meetings

▶ Meets regularly with the leader's team for prayer, to discuss the group's progress and development, and to brainstorm

▶ Provides refreshments (or organizes the group members to provide refreshments) as outlined in the group covenant

Developing a Group Covenant

1. The reason our group exists is:

   _____.

2. Our specific group goals include:

   _____.

3. We meet ___ time(s) a month, and this covenant will be in effect for ___ weeks/months. At the end of the covenant period, we will evaluate our progress and growth.

4. We will meet on _____ (day of week), from _____ A.M./P.M. to _____ A.M./P.M.

5. Our meetings will be at _____ (place[s]).

6. We will use _____ as a basis for study or training.

7. We will agree on one or more of the following disciplines:
   ❏ Attendance: We will be here whenever possible.
   ❏ Ownership: We will share responsibility for the group and our goals.
   ❏ Confidentiality: We agree to keep here whatever is shared here.
   ❏ Accountability: We give permission to the other group members to hold us accountable for goals we set for ourselves.
   ❏ Accessibility: We permit each other to call whenever we are in need—even in the middle of the night. My phone: _____.

8. Other possible ground rules:
   ❏ Food and snacks (who's responsible for bringing what)
   ❏ Child care
   ❏ Group leadership: single leader with apprentice, or rotating leadership
   ❏ Our plan for growth and multiplication:

   _____

9. Additional issues to consider in creating your group
   covenant:
   ☐ Open or closed: Will our group be open (with new
     members continuously recruited or dropping in),
     closed (not open after the third meeting), or a combi-
     nation of both (open during certain times—i.e., at the
     beginning of a new book or a new year)?
   ☐ Service and outreach: Our plan for service (to the
     church, our neighborhood, or our community) and for
     reaching out to those outside the church needs to be
     discussed and developed (additional ideas and infor-
     mation can found in session 6).
   ☐ Fun and recreation: To round out a group and keep it
     vibrant, it's advisable to plan fun nights and recre-
     ational outings on occasion. Many have found it useful
     to add a fun time every 6–8 meetings.

Signed: _____

YOU CAN LEAD DYNAMIC, LIFE-CHANGING SMALL-GROUP BIBLE STUDIES!

We hope you've enjoyed this NavPress study guide. Good materials are only part of what makes a successful and fulfilling small-group experience. That's why NavPress is pleased to announce PILGRIMAGE/NAVPRESS SMALL-GROUP TRAINING SEMINARS.

Whether you've led groups for years or are just starting out, PILGRIMAGE/NAVPRESS SMALL-GROUP TRAINING will help you create and lead the kind of groups that foster life-changing spiritual growth.

In just 7 hours you'll learn:

▶ "Hands-on" small-group training techniques from the leading experts in North America

▶ The 7 essential skills every effective small-group leader needs

▶ How groups can specialize in worship, evangelism, discipleship, and emotional healing

▶ How small groups can help entire church bodies increase in love for one another

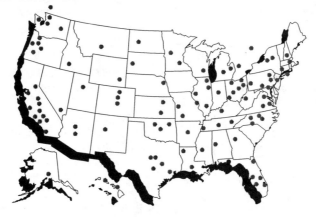

PILGRIMAGE/NAVPRESS SMALL-GROUP TRAINING SEMINARS are held at hundreds of locations all over North America. Call 1-800-GRPS-R-US for more information about seminars available in your area.

1-800-477-7787

PILGRIMAGE
NAVPRESS

SMALL-GROUP MATERIALS FROM NAVPRESS

BIBLE STUDY SERIES

DESIGN FOR DISCIPLESHIP
GOD IN YOU
GOD'S DESIGN FOR THE FAMILY
INSTITUTE OF BIBLICAL
  COUNSELING Series
LEARNING TO LOVE Series

LIFECHANGE
RADICAL RELATIONSHIPS
SPIRITUAL DISCIPLINES
STUDIES IN CHRISTIAN LIVING
THINKING THROUGH DISCIPLESHIP

TOPICAL BIBLE STUDIES

Becoming a Woman of Excellence
Becoming a Woman of Freedom
Becoming a Woman of Prayer
Becoming a Woman of Purpose
The Blessing Study Guide
Homemaking
Intimacy with God
Loving Your Husband

Loving Your Wife
A Mother's Legacy
Praying From God's Heart
Surviving Life in the Fast Lane
To Run and Not Grow Tired
To Walk and Not Grow Weary
What God Does When Men Pray
When the Squeeze Is On

BIBLE STUDIES WITH COMPANION BOOKS

Bold Love
Daughters of Eve
The Discipline of Grace
The Feminine Journey
Inside Out
The Masculine Journey
The Practice of Godliness
The Pursuit of Holiness

Secret Longings of the Heart
Spiritual Disciplines
Tame Your Fears
Transforming Grace
Trusting God
What Makes a Man?
The Wounded Heart

RESOURCES

Brothers!
Discipleship Journal's Best
  Small-Group Ideas
How to Build a Small Groups Ministry
How to Lead Small Groups
Jesus Cares for Women
The Navigator Bible Studies
  Handbook

The Small Group Leaders
  Training Course
Topical Memory System
  (KJV/NIV and NASB/NKJV)
Topical Memory System:
  Life Issues